THE
TROUT
DIARIES

A year of fly-fishing in New Zealand

DEREK GRZELEWSKI

David Bateman

Text © Derek Grzelewski, 2011
Typographical design © David Bateman Ltd, 2011

Published in 2011 by David Bateman Ltd
30 Tarndale Grove, Albany, Auckland, New Zealand
www.batemanpublishing.co.nz

Distributed in USA by Stackpole Books
5067 Ritter Road, Mechanicsburg, PA 17055, USA

Reprinted 2011

ISBN 978-1-86953-724-1

Book design & maps: Nick Turzynski, redinc., Auckland
Front jacket illustration: Errol McLeary
All photographs by Derek Grzelewski (www.derekgrzelewski.com)
except colour section 2, page 4: David Lloyd
Fly illustrations: Johnny Groome (www.johnnygroomeart.vc.net.nz)
All flies by Ian Cole (www.iancole.co.nz)
Printed in China by Everbest Printing Co. Ltd

Contents

For Ada, lost and found

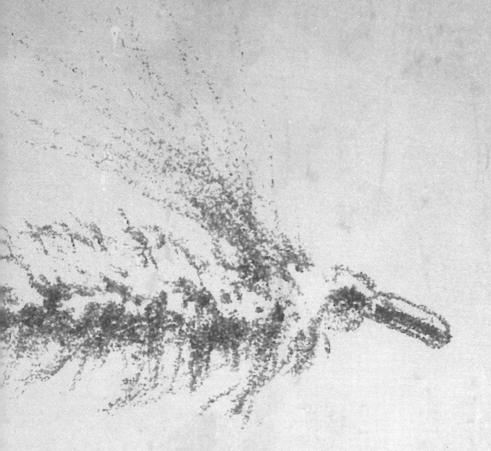

'I fish because . . . in a world where most men seem to spend their lives doing things they hate, my fishing is at once an endless source of delight and an act of small rebellion; because trout do not lie or cheat and cannot be bought or bribed or impressed by power, but respond only to quietude and humility and endless patience; because I suspect that men are going along this way for the last time, and I for one don't want to waste the trip . . . '

ROBERT TRAVER, *Anatomy of a Fisherman*

'All good things — trout as well as eternal salvation — come by grace and grace comes by art and art does not come easy.'

NORMAN MACLEAN, *A River Runs Through It*

'I only cast when I have to.'

MARC HERTAULT

THE CREEK WAS A PERFECT TROUT STREAM, a staircase
of pools and riffles, defined and stable, remote and little known,
brimming with potential and promise. It cut deep into the Otago
farmland, and the banks that framed it were like miniature
escarpments. Sheep had worn tracks along both edges, affording
easy walking and excellent vantage points from which to search
the water. It was the kind of place where you'd expect trophy
brown trout to be sitting high in the water in their prime lies,
undisturbed and feeding eagerly.

My angling compadre, David Lloyd, and I had never fished this
creek before, but we were eager to explore new waters. The past
three days of our annual early-season pilgrimage had been the best
we'd ever had on our favourite 'River X'. The fish were active and
plentiful, and almost embarrassingly easy in what is usually tough
water. Each day had been better than the one before, and we knew
we could not sustain this level of intensity. Our exceptionally good
fortune would inevitably come to an end, so we decided to pocket
our winnings and change venues, start afresh on new water, with a
clean scoreboard and innocent hopes.

The weather, too, was deteriorating. After nearly a week of
sunshine, a slab of bruise-coloured clouds shuttered the
sky, heralding heavy rain and rivers in spate. This was the calm
before the storm, surely our last day of fishing on this trip. Still,
despite the heavy skies, this gem of a creek had us buzzing with
anticipation. There had to be trout here, surely not as plentiful as
in our River X, but that would be fine by us. We were after quality,
not numbers. The creek was a dream and we were living it. It was
only a matter of time, short time, before we found a feeding fish.

We walked slowly, our eyes X-raying the water, following feed
lines and the seams of colour change along the bottom, dissecting
the fast broken riffles, looking for what David called the 'soft
shadowy shapes'. Our rods were rigged up for all possibilities,
David's with double nymphs and a white yarn indicator, mine with
a light taper line and a dry fly, the first-choice Parachute Adams.
The creek unfolded before us like a good tale, one turn at a time,
and we had it to ourselves, all of it, all the way to the forest, a long
day's fishing away. Our imaginations worked overtime, conjuring
double-figure fish and screaming reels. Surely, if such things were
to happen, this was the place and time.

But, strangely, we were not seeing fish. Not a single one. We were not spooking any, either, which was the more disturbing of the two. Hunters who are flushing out their quarry are at least getting close to it. They can hone their skills, walk more stealthily, look further ahead. But not seeing the quarry at all dilutes the concentration and makes the attention wander. It also brings about a peculiar kind of heavy-hearted despair and doubt. Lots of doubt.

Was it us or the fish? Were they simply not here, or were we not seeing them? Had someone fished the creek today already? Had the water been polluted by some upstream dairy farm, so that it only looked perfect but was in fact lifeless?

In creeks like this it is unreasonable to expect fish in every pool. This kind of water falls into a category which the guidebooks describe with 'long walks required between fish'. So we walked, and looked, hour after hour. We ate lunch in silence, sitting on a high bank overlooking yet another perfect pool, never taking our eyes off the water and never seeing a thing that even remotely looked like a trout.

At times like these, you begin to think that, completely without reason and despite all past experiences, you are never going to catch another fish. Botched presentations, refusals and missed takes are all fine, part of the game. But not getting even a single opportunity for all the miles we'd already put in was just too disheartening. Especially on the water that promised so much.

I was beginning to lose interest, walking faster and more carelessly, paying less and less attention to the water, which in sight-fishing is the beginning of the end. Then David grabbed my sleeve, his rod tip pointing up and across the creek to a feed line beneath the opposite bank.

'There,' he said almost reverently, 'a rise, if I ever saw one.'

Then to himself he added: 'And why am I whispering?'

It was as if the sun had come out, in an instant changing our internal weather, dispelling the gloom, lighting everything with vibrant colours. A miracle had just occurred, banishing all doubt and despair. We had found a fish, and it was feeding. Right now, there was nothing more we asked of the world.

It was a clean emerger rise, with no part of the fish breaking the surface, only a soft dimple and a few air bubbles. I tied on a Cul de Canard emerger and offered the rod to David.

'No, I'd only fuck it up,' he said. 'You go. No pressure though.'

It was nearly four o'clock, and in all likelihood we'd not find another fish today. No pressure indeed.

The day was still windless and I had a #4 double-taper line on a #6 rod, a trick I'd learnt from one of the old-timers on our River X. The rig requires you to adjust your casting

> *The rise was another soft dimple,*
> *as if a drop of rain had fallen into the*
> *water. But as I lifted the rod I felt the*
> *weight of the fish, solid and alive.*

technique, but done right it is capable of unsurpassedly delicate presentation, especially with a dry fly. I waited for the fish to rise again. It did and I had its position pinpointed.

For a moment I thought it would be interesting to have been wearing one of those heart-rate monitors that are all the rage in aerobic fitness training. Judging by the pounding in my ears, the thing would surely be spiking in the red zone, right up there with an uphill sprint. I took a deep steadying breath, let all the nonsense fall away and began to cast.

I made the first cast deliberately short, both to straighten the line and to better judge the distance. Then, with all the skills and calm I could muster, I placed the tiny emerger into the feed line, a good metre ahead of the fish.

The rise was another soft dimple, as if a drop of rain had fallen into the water. But as I lifted the rod I felt the weight of the fish, solid and alive. David yelled an inarticulate cry of victory, the fish leaped, flashed silver in the overcast light, then tore off upstream and took another big air, shaking itself head to tail with fury. It hit the surface of the pool with a flop and the line went slack.

It took a few more pounding heartbeats for the senses to register, then to accept that the fish was gone. The intensity of the moment was punctured. I sat on the bank — it is easier to shake sitting down — and watched the slack line drifting past me. I pulled it in and saw that the emerger was still on, its punk stem brilliantined with mucus. The fish had not broken me off, it simply shook out the hook on the jump.

There was not much to say, but we both agreed to call it a day, and walked back to the truck, each lost in his own silence. It was only later that night, by the fire in a classic rural Otago pub, that we dared to talk about what had happened.

'You know, of all the fish we've caught, or tried to catch — ever

— that was the one I'll remember most,' David said. 'Today we struck pure gold, a few pounds of it. Forget about trophies and numbers. That was what it is all about: magic moments like that.'

Outside it was already raining heavily, and the storm gusts sounded like fistfuls of lead shot thrown against the windows. The fishing was over for a week or more, but that did not matter. David was right. A dozen fish would not have made the day more memorable. The magic moment was earned and ours, a trophy to keep, and a reason to walk more riverbanks in the hope of one day living it again.

Trout, and the rivers and lakes where they are found, have a way of drawing the fly-fisher in, deeply and inextricably. What begins as a weekend hobby soon becomes a way of life. It dictates the kind of car you buy, the colour of your clothes, the roads you choose to travel to places, the people you spend most time with, sometimes even the jobs you take. Once the rivers lure you in deeply enough, they redefine your personal geography, too, so that it's no longer based on towns, cities and roads that connect them, but on rivers, lakes, watersheds and directions of flow. At this stage, every time you cross a bridge you cannot help but to slow down even if for the quickest of looks, even if you have no fishing gear with you — though by now it's likely your rod and vest are as inseparable from your vehicle as the jack and the spare wheel.

Yet despite, or perhaps because of, their abiding allure, trout themselves remain mysterious and unpredictable creatures, making the fishing for them a complex and open-ended affair. My friend and longtime fly-fishing mentor, Wanaka guide Ian Cole — a man who spends more time on the water than just about anyone else I know, and who has converted his entire walk-in wardrobe into a storage place for rods and fly-tying materials — once told me: 'The more I fish for trout, the less I know about them.' He did not have to add 'and the more I want to know'. That went without saying.

I, too, have been drawn into the pursuit of trout — slowly at first, flirtatiously almost, until over some ten years ago I found myself spending so much time on the water that I decided I might as well become a guide; turn the passion into a dream job.

This, I now realise, was a mistake, because good guiding has little to do with being a good fisherman, and people who say that 'the worst day's fishing is still better than the best day at work' have clearly not fully experienced either.

INTRODUCTION

Guiding can be both extremely rewarding and it can numb your soul. A guide is at once a paid companion and a confidant, a cook, chauffeur and paramedic, a fish and human psychologist, a problem-solver and sometimes just a straight-out trout pimp. Don't get me wrong. I'm not against guiding, not any more, though at one point I used to think that catching a fish while being guided was like hearing a punch line without the rest of the joke, a moral without the story. Some of my closest friends are guides, and they are as fine human beings as they are expert anglers. They have to be, because out of a hundred or so days in the season there are only a few when it all comes together perfectly. For the rest of the time a good guide has to be both a compassionate nurse and a miracle maker.

Ultimately, though, the point of fly-fishing for trout is to guide ourselves through the complexities of the sport, its highs and lows, joys and frustrations, nuances and mysteries. In this journey trout is more a direction than a goal, because no matter how much you learn and how good a fly-fisher you become, there are always surprises, both those that delight and those that humble. And still there is more, always more, because trout and their ways can never be fully known, and for that, too, we must be eternally grateful.

Ever since Zane Grey, the American writer of romance westerns, fly-fished in New Zealand in the 1920s and declared the country to be the *Angler's Eldorado*, trout enthusiasts from around the world — members of what Izaak Walton called the 'Brotherhood of the Angle' — have been making pilgrimages to the rivers and lakes of both islands, and for a good reason. Nine decades after Grey's visits, New Zealand remains the country of trout, a dream destination for anyone with a passion for a fly rod, even if all too often New Zealanders still need foreigners to remind them of that.

There may be bigger fish elsewhere — Oregon steelheads, the sea-run trout of Patagonia — but for sheer diversity and quality of fishing for wild brown and rainbow trout, New Zealand remains unsurpassed. This is why the town of Gore, at the bottom of the South Island, built a monument to the fish and proclaimed itself the brown trout capital of the world, while Turangi, where the Tongariro River enters Lake Taupo in the North Island, did the same with rainbow trout. To us New Zealanders, who favour the understated over the bombastic — Ed Hillary's 'We knocked the bastard off' over Neil Armstrong's 'one giant leap for mankind' — such boasting may seem naff and pretentious, mere tourism promoters' rant. With any luck, one day we may finally get the fact that the boast is itself an understatement.

All it takes is someone like David Lloyd to tell the story of his
father, a lifelong angler who fished the ponds and streams of
England with regularity and passion. He was a competent caster
and an avid fly tier, but he had never caught a trout over 3 lbs.
What in New Zealand we would call 'just a wee fella, about 3 lbs' for
David's father would have been a trophy, a fish to remember for
the rest of his days.

Still, even with such reminders, in New Zealand it is too easy to
take the exceptional for normal, the gift for the given; to assume
that the rivers and the trout as we know them will still be there
tomorrow, and that we will be here to enjoy them. It often requires
something that shakes our world out of its comfort and patterns of
predictability — a collision, an accident or illness — to show us the
impermanence of things and how foolish it is to assume anything
at all. For me, it happened on a river with Henry Spencer.

There is a vagrant population of fly-fishermen and women
in New Zealand — retirees, life stylers, most of them seasonal
migrants from overseas — and if you roam and fish the country
long enough you invariably begin to bump into them as they
follow the season to wherever the fishing is best at the time.
Some people call them trout bums. I've come to call them — us
— trout bohemians, and Henry Spencer was certainly one of the
movement's exemplars.

I first met him on the Eglinton River in Fiordland. He was
a quiet and gentle man in his early sixties, private and self-
content, immaculately decked out in a crisp sea-blue shirt and
matching tan-coloured waders and vest, both of which seemed
tailor-made, and happier on a river than in any other place he
could imagine himself to be. After a calm morning, a nor'wester
had kicked in, quickly turning into a downstream howler, making
spotting fish and casting impossible. I was coming down the river
and back to my camper when I met Henry, who, far from being
frustrated by the headwind, simply turned around, changed
his dry-fly and nymph rig to a streamer — the ubiquitous olive
Woolly Bugger — and began to fish downstream, with the wind
and the current.

As I passed, I invited him for a drink in my camper, and
eventually he succumbed, though only after the wind grew so
strong it became impossible not just to cast but even to keep
the fly line in the water. In the camper, nosed into the gale and
rocking like a boxer looking for an opening, we drank Ethiopian
coffee and talked fishermen's talk, about places, rivers and flies,
about the most memorable fish.

Henry never said much about himself, though I gleaned he was
a retired teacher from somewhere in the American Midwest, that
he was a widower and that his two daughters were happily married.
I always thought of him as a *Dead Poets Society* kind of teacher, though
calmer and less flamboyant than the Robin Williams character.
He drew a tight circle around his private life, but he delighted in
debating anything to do with trout, rivers and fly-fishing, and
always he had things to say, good and thought-through things that
come not from books but from first-hand experience.

For him, New Zealand was the greatest find of his life, a new
world of fishing possibilities, and laughingly he talked of himself
as the trout Columbus discovering his own personal *Terra Trutta*.
Over the years, I'd bump into Henry two or three times a season:
on a West Coast spring creek, on the Buller River near St Arnaud,
on the Mataura in Athol, once or twice on the Tongariro. Then,
last year, as we sat on our green fold-out chairs on the bank of the
Inangahua River, outside Reefton, Henry, unusually for him, told
me some more about himself. The news was not good.

Only a couple of months earlier, he said, he'd been
diagnosed with a terminal cancer. The medical specialists advised
chemotherapy, though more as a delay of the inevitable than a cure.
They gave him six months; a year if he was lucky. Henry's face was
pale as he talked, but his eyes were still bright — perhaps not with
their usual gentle fire but with some fierce inner resolve. He had
organised his affairs, he told me, tied up all the loose ends, sold his
possessions, written up a will. But he would not subject himself to
the chemo. He would not end his life vegetating on a life-support
system, waiting for some merciful person to turn it off. No, he
would end it here, on a river in New Zealand, and he would fish
every day until the Reaper came, and when the moment arrived he
would be ready for it and would welcome it, knowing that he had
lived well and did what he loved until the end.

He even wrote a letter in case a stranger found him dead on a
riverbank. One copy he carried in his vest with his fishing licence;
the other he taped to the dashboard of his forest-green Subaru.
The letter, he said, explained that it was all right, that this was what
he had planned.

'Don't want any poor fella to panic or blame himself,' Henry
said. 'There is nothing anyone can do, including me.'

What can you say to such an announcement? Consolations
seemed trivial, reassurances empty. I said I was sorry (what a useless
word that is) and that if he had to, this was certainly a fine way to
go. I looked towards the river, hoping for something, a rising fish

perhaps, something that would break the gloom, offer a diversion. But the river was quiet, and the silence heavy, and we sat without any more words, nursing our drinks until the night came.

That last encounter with Henry left me rattled and restless. It sent me re-examining my own ways and priorities, and above all looking at the long list of 'things to do before you die', many of which had to do with fly-fishing. There were famous and not-so-famous rivers I wanted to explore at particular times of the season, and people I wanted to fish them with. These trips and visits, long and often promised and discussed, had somehow always managed to get postponed in the knowledge that there would surely be another time, perhaps a better time, after we dealt with what was immediate and seemingly important.

But what if there was no more time, no next year, future season, better weather? What if, as in Henry's case, each day, each river, each cast or fish might be the last one? What would that do to the way I fished? The way I lived? These thoughts were not morbid but sobering. They put my days on a river into sharper relief, gave them a kind of *carpe diem* intensity.

Thus the idea for this diary was born. Where would I go, what would I do, I asked myself, if, like Henry, I had this one last season to fish? It did not mean I'd fish all day every day, confusing, as it were, mileage with meaning. I learned long ago that the hours we put in to an activity do not always translate into the intensity of experience. Nor is the size or number of fish caught a qualifying factor. This was more about collecting trophies of a different kind: sensory snapshots of unforgettable fish, moments of riverside magic like the single trout on the nameless creek I hooked and lost with David, moments that never fade from memory; the kind of trout experience that puts a goofy smile on your face or makes your eyes glaze over into that thousand-yard stare every time you think of them.

Living in New Zealand, I was already in the best possible place on the planet to conduct such an experiment, but which rivers and places would I choose? Which events in the trout calendar would I want to witness and participate in?

Though I've fished a lot and often, that elegant circular continuity to the trout's year had so far eluded me, and closing that circle would make a worthwhile quest. It has to do with the life cycles of the trout's food, the seasons and spawning patterns, the way a river can be full of feeding fish one month, and another be completely empty, and with the knowing which month was which. At its heart, fly-fishing is as much about understanding trout as catching them, about solving riverside riddles and glimpsing a greater unknown that is far more satisfying than the relatively simple act of hauling in a lump of meat.

Silently thanking Henry for this jolt of inspiration, I made an inventory of my gear, restocked my fly boxes, studied my maps and began to pencil in tentative dates. Then, of course, life intervened with its deadlines, commitments and other must-dos, and for a while it seemed I was back to the old patterns and routines, as if the 'get up and live' edict Henry had unknowingly given me had never happened. Yet fate had already written my own 'Mack truck' experiences into the trout diary, though I did not see them coming or have any indication of their collision course. You never do. They always seem to blindside you when you least expect them.

The season was only two weeks away, opening-day fever already palpable in the local tackle shop, and I was still making plans. I thought I'd let that short-lived fever pass, as I always did, before heading out on my first adventure. But then, walking my Airedale terrier Mops along the fishermen's track that parallels my home river, the Clutha, I saw the *Deleatidium* mayfly hatch, brown and dainty. And I watched the trout, still famished from spawning, rise to gorge on them so eagerly they did not seem to go back down under after taking each fly but surfed the current with their mouths open, their golden-brown bodies partly above the water at all times.

I thought of Henry. He would not wait, plan around the weather, the conditions, the possibility of crowds. He would simply go and fish, regardless. Right now, he would be trotting to the car to get his gear, assembling the rod on his way back to where the fish were rising, knowing that the trout would rise again another day but that he might not necessarily be there to see it. The clock was ticking, and he was only too aware of it. The time to fish was now, not at some future date pencilled into the diary and subject to this, that and the other contingency and constraint. And so I began packing my camper, and later that night I called a friend with an offer I knew he could not refuse.

October

WHEN I MET UP WITH SEAGULL TWO weeks later, on a sunny spring morning in Wanaka, he looked more like a lost albatross than a spunky gull. He was an old though nowadays rarely seen friend — a farmer's son and a practical kind of guy who once, working on track maintenance in Fiordland during the roar, lured a stag to within metres of him by imitating the animal's haughty call with a chainsaw. 'Seagull' was a boarding-school nickname, bestowed on account of a ravenous appetite that spurred him to raid his schoolmates' lunchboxes.

Right now, though, Seagull was seriously down on his luck. In quick succession he had been through a marriage break-up and a heart attack (at thirty-five), both of which led to an over-dependence on antidepressants. Unable to break out of gloomy introspective moods, he was re-examining the hand life had dealt him and struggling to find a trump card.

'What say we go for a few days to fish the Catlins?' I said.

'Catlins!' Seagull's face lit up at the sound of the name. It was where he had grown up, where his grandfather had logged and his family once farmed. The very name was a recall to his boyhood playground, to a time when the world was young, possibilities endless and he could do no wrong.

His bags were still packed from his latest misadventure — a ski-touring expedition in Mt Aspiring National Park which had ended when he and his companion were caught in an avalanche, dragged and buried nearly a kilometre down the slope, and barely managed to dig themselves out from the snowy pulp that set about them like concrete. Going to fish his childhood waters, where he and his brothers used to haunt the irrigation ditches, trolling spinners as they walked and hooking what would today surely pass for trophy brown trout, promised to bring back a modicum of sanity into his world.

We stocked up on food and within hours we were driving east. That night we saw a sea lion and fossicked for paua at low tide. We camped in a grove of wind-lashed fuchsia, and I could not wait for the morning and the rivers Seagull had told me so much about during the drive, but which I'd never fished.

I once read a magazine story which lauded the delights of early-season *Coloburiscus* hatches in the Catlins. *Coloburiscus* is one of the largest of our mayfly species, and its nymph has an unusual feeding strategy of filtering out food particles with the long hairs that grow on its legs. If, like me, you are used to fishing with dries that are almost too small to tie on the tippet without glasses, and are barely if not at all visible once on the water, casting a #12 Colly that is as big as a small butterfly and floats like a cork seems too good to be true. I only ever encountered these nymphs once before, on the Waiau River between Te Anau and Manapouri, and I had nothing big enough in my fly box to match the hatch of this mayfly on steroids. On that memorable occasion I had overstocked on flies in a local tackle shop — beautifully tied Kakahi Queens and Dad's Favourites, sulphur and tan, all obscenely super-size — and they had been living in my fly box ever since, as I had had neither the courage nor the opportunity to use them again. The Catlins rivers, I hoped, would finally let them see some action.

The area known as the Catlins — the South Island's south-easternmost coastline and hinterland — stretches between the mouths of the Clutha and the Mataura Rivers, but I like to think of it as the coast between two lighthouses, at Nugget and Waipapa Points, perhaps because the two structures symbolise the precarious nature of human existence in this part of the country.

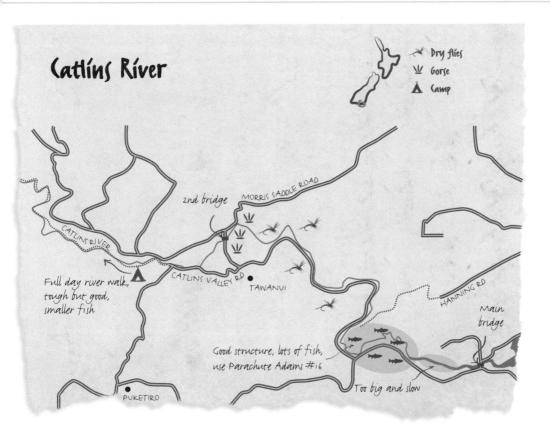

The lighthouses stand as pillars at the land's end, concrete fortresses against the Roaring Forties and the wind that makes the crowns of trees grow sideways, like plumes of smoke.

Topographically, the Catlins look like a hand, its fingers pointing at the ocean. In this imaginary hand, the palm is the interior, much of it reserved as Catlins Forest Park, each finger a hilly ridge, each fingertip a sea-cliff, each gap between the fingers a river valley widening into an estuary. Much of the Catlins is still covered in trees. Podocarps and beeches make up the rainforest, which in places comes right down to the ocean, and which has about it the same moist luxuriance as the forests on the West Coast or in Fiordland.

These woods once supported a frontier logging industry, with makeshift ponga-and-tussock-thatch settlements, after which came the farmers, wresting pockets of land from the bush. Even today, some of the hill pastures — as verdant as a golf course but littered with stumps and weathered timber — look like a short-back-and-sides haircut, with mops of forest crowning the topmost hills and ridges.

Paddocks and forest meet along ragged edges, as if the farmers had only just downed their land-clearing tools and left. Seagull told me that in some cases they probably have. Like yellow wildfire, thickets of gorse threaten to overrun all open ground. After twelve years of dawn-to-dusk toil, Seagull's family had sold their farm and left for easier pastures. Between the forest and the gorse, in the full blast of subantarctic weather, they found the Catlins just too tough to handle.

In the morning we headed inland, following the lower Catlins River, crossing hillocky farmland towards the forest. The river twisted through stands of beech, mirroring the trees in its tea-coloured water. We stopped and peered into the river from behind a barricade of gorse. In the glare of the overcast day the water had a metallic sheen, and along its smooth surface slow leisurely trout rises drifted downstream like smoke rings. I turned to say something to Seagull, something wise about the *Coloburiscus* mayfly and the nature of the Universe, but he was already back at the camper, pulling out his rod tube, rigging up with all the haste of a fireman called to an emergency.

I gave Seagull one of my prized Kakahi Queens, and he tied it on and eyed the nearest fish. By now we saw that the trout were rising with an almost metronomic precision and frequency, one rise ring barely dissipating before the next had formed. Seagull cast, the fly landed with acceptable accuracy and the uniform flow of the river meant that line drag, which can make an artificial fly move at odds with the current and its natural look-alikes, was never going to be an issue. The fly looked *good* on the water, sitting high, its hackles bending the surface film just so. Our eyes darted from the fish to the approaching fly to the fish again, waiting for the inevitable as the distance between the two was shrinking fast.

The fish rose, took a natural, let the beautiful and well-ginked Kakahi Queen drift by, then took something else immediately behind it. Surely, it must have seen Seagull's fly. Maybe it was just a matter of bad timing. I've seen this on the Mataura often enough. As the metronomic tempo of rising trout reaches a certain speed, as the fish gets into a porpoising motion of a swimmer doing butterfly stroke, gulping not air but flies, there is a rhythm to its takes and an angler has to synchronise with this beat and present a fly precisely as the fish is coming up, or his offering will be ignored.

Seagull made a few more casts, some of them landing a little close, but the fish never spooked. It continued to rise, and at times we could hear the snap of its jaws, sounding like a gentle clap of wet hands, as it slurped another fly. Only it was never our *Coloburiscus* imitation, even though at times the stately Kakahi Queen seemed to get in the way of the fish taking the naturals.

For just such moments I carry with me a small sieve, about the size of a tea strainer. I carry it about in secret, well-buried in the pockets of my vest, because among the uninitiated the sight of such a device tends to spawn pranky comments, like whether fishing with a sieve is legal in New Zealand, or if this is my idea of a landing net.

Well, it is a landing net of sorts, though not for the fish but for the surface insects which, nearly weightless and floating with a fast current, are almost impossible to catch by hand. Maybe not impossible, but time consuming, and when the fish are rising time is precious and I'd rather spend it catching fish, not insects. I leave that to those gangly, butterfly-net toting types with a long string of academic credits in entomology.

I left Seagull by the fish and walked downstream to where the pool was tapering off into a riffle, knelt down and held the sieve against the current. When I lifted it, the riddle of the fish refusing our Kakahi Queen was instantly solved: the mayflies, bedraggled and semi-translucent against the steel mesh of the sieve, were not the meaty *Coloburiscus* at all but the more common Blue Duns, pale little grey ghosts when seen fluttering against sunlight and so perfectly imitated by one of the all-time classic flies, the #16 Parachute Adams.

I shared this revelation with Seagull, and he changed the fly and cast. The Adams landed a bit off to the side. The fish took another natural from the feed line, then darted cross-current almost a metre and took the Parachute. Seagull struck, a little early, felt the fish, and then the fly pulled out and all ten metres of line twanged towards his face. Considering all the gorse and matagouri around us, this augured a mighty tangle.

With good reflexes, Seagull never let the line reach him, back-casting it instead, letting it straighten behind, then, on instinct or perhaps because there were really no other alternatives, he cast the fly back into the feed line.

Instantly, the fish appeared on the surface and took, and Seagull hooked it, this time for good. Yes, I thought, this is the kind of fish we want. Patient and forgiving.

For the rest of the day we walked the river, picking off all the rising fish we could find. I lost count of the number. They were all relatively small, none bigger than 3 lb, but they all took our dries like there was no tomorrow.

Seagull, too, seemed to have sensed what a special gift we had been handed. His introspective gloom was lifting. There were fish in the river, and they were happy to see our flies, and for now it was all that mattered.

As we were setting up camp that evening, I heard Seagull humming to himself. He stopped a man passing by in a ute, and the two fell into an easy farmer-to-farmer conversation: about the lambing, the Catlins weather — how it came in violent cycles of storm and sunshine, how it bent around the hills, sparing some, pounding others. The lambing season, harshest in years, was nearing its end, and the soggy paddocks above the river were dotted with cutesy youngsters, some prancing, others standing by their mothers, looking in confusion at this strange world into which they had just arrived.

The pastoral scenes stirred boyhood memories in Seagull's mind. 'We used to get lambing leave from boarding school to help our parents on the farm,' he said as we ate our supper. 'An extra ten days at the end of the August holidays, though holidays they were definitely not.'

The farm would be divided among all the able-bodied men, he said, then each would patrol his beat, an ovine midwife on a farm bike. It was so cold they stitched possum skins over the handlebars for mittens.

'We had mainly Romney sheep,' Seagull went on, 'and they are notoriously difficult lambers.' Some mothers would abandon their offspring, and there were a lot of stillborns.

'When you found an orphan you looked for a ewe with a dead lamb,' he said. 'You'd skin the dead one, make a little fleece vest out of its skin and dress the orphan in it, so that through smell the ewe would accept it as her own.'

The lambing season was always a slow, muddy marathon of worry and sleep deprivation, punctuated with bursts of what Seagull called the 'Southland sprint' — a run-for-your-life dash in gumboots, yellow PVC raincoat and over-trousers from a moving four-wheeler across spongy paddocks to tackle a runaway lamb.

'You can see why Southlanders revere rugby,' Seagull grinned. 'Here, tackling and scoring tries are practical, everyday skills.'

That night, by our small campfire of dry beech wood, it occurred to me we were at the birthplace of the 'Southern Man' legend. Nearby, on a Department of Conservation sign that informed us we were in the Catlins State Forest, someone had tested the spread of his shotgun at close range, and an image of a farmer, stoically driving a quad bike against a brief but violent storm that sent hail like peppercorns bouncing off his ruddy cheeks, was still fresh in my memory.

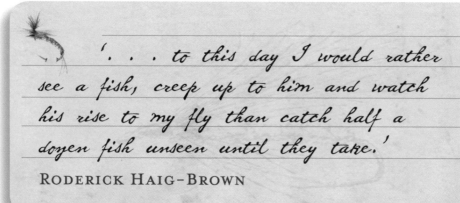

'. . . to this day I would rather see a fish, creep up to him and watch his rise to my fly than catch half a dozen fish unseen until they take.'

RODERICK HAIG-BROWN

Seagull, always a good actor, broke into a tale which smacked of the memorable Speight's beer advertisements.

'My old man once bought a ton of Speight's. It was on special in Dunedin,' he said, staring thoughtfully into the flames. 'Had to keep the Land Rover outside. The crates filled up the whole garage.'

We gazed some more into the fire before I dutifully picked up my expected role.

'And? Did the beer last long?' I asked.

'Not as long as you'd think,' Seagull replied. 'Mind you, we all helped.'

I lowered my voice to a low grumble and said: 'Good on ya, mate.'

In the morning, as we were finishing our coffee, sitting on camping chairs right by the river, Seagull spotted the first rise of the day, a gentle sip on the edge of sunlight and willow shade.

'We'd better carpe diem,' he said. 'Or make it trout-a-diem.'

We fished until another crisp sundown, changing flies only when they began to unravel, and never once did we go back to floating a *Coloburiscus* to a feeding trout. Not that it mattered. Not that anything else mattered.

These were our godsend days in the Catlins, and we both knew it. Indeed, I would pass through here two more times, later in the season, and each time I'd catch an odd fish, but never see such prolific hatches, and the days were never as good as those I passed there with Seagull.

As for my collection of Kakahi Queens and Dad's Favourites, elegant and bristling with purpose, they'd have to wait for another day, a day on an as-tough-as-it gets West Coast spring creek.

#12 Colly Emerger

I'm willing to bet that, like me, you have a river of your dreams, a place that comes first to your mind whenever you think 'fly-fishing'. It may be a memory snapshot of somewhere you've already been or a mental composite of everything you find most appealing in your pursuit of angling perfection.

Picture it for a moment. What is the river like?

What size, with what backdrop, in what country? Does it have long, smooth glides where rise-rings take forever to dissipate, or is it fast and boisterous, with plenty of big rocks for rainbows to hold against? Is it an easy, ego-pampering water à la Timaru Creek or a humbling test like the lower Tongariro, where massive browns do not even spook any more and regard you with contempt? Whenever I closed my eyes I could see my river clearly, but only this spring I discovered that it actually existed, and that it had a name. I also got to fish it for all of three days. Talk about vision becoming a reality!

The river is called La Fontaine, and it seeps out of swampy paddocks on the West Coast, two hours north of the glaciers, near the farming settlement of Hari Hari. It is tempting to think that it might have been named after the writer Gary LaFontaine, who, as one journalist noted in a 2002 obituary, 'was a fly-fisherman — in much the same way Albert Einstein was a mathematician'. LaFontaine's books — *Trout Flies: Proven Patterns*, *Caddisflies*, and *The Dry Fly: New Angles* — are classics in their field. But it's more likely —

certain, in fact — that the river carries the name of another scribe, the Frenchman Jean de La Fontaine, a conjurer of magic and fables. Such an association seems fitting for a dream river like this.

I had been meaning to explore it for years, and never did, but, in line with my new-season credo, this was the year of fulfilling such promises. David Lloyd was back in town, and one sunny day in late October we set off in my camper up the coast.

David has been fishing with me for a few years now, commuting to New Zealand from Hong Kong for a week or two several times a year. Most times I'd pick him up at the airport and we'd hit the ground running, going from river to river, camping out every night, returning to civilisation just in time for his boarding call. Our longest day fishing stands at eighteen hours — dawn to summer dusk and beyond — and if New Zealand lay further south, garnering more daylight, I'm sure David would want to fish around the clock. His attitude towards trout makes the word 'keen' an understatement. It has also earned him a nickname: 'Just one more cast'.

By the time of our departure for the coast we'd already had a week's fishing on our favourite River X. It had been a memorable trip. Sight-fishing to eager browns, the solitude and the luxury of having had the river to ourselves had raised our standards, honed the expectations. Thus we arrived in Hari Hari a little too cocky, perhaps: two self-professed experts ready to kick butt. The La Fontaine browns would see to it that we did not delude ourselves for long.

La Fontaine Stream is a river-sized spring creek, with fat weedbeds waving in the current over clear patches of light gravel and sand, all of which makes for rather good spotting. David and I delight in sight-fishing, now almost to the exclusion of any other style, and the 'See no fish, make no cast' precept has become our *modus operandi*. We are happy to walk for miles just looking for the moments of magic this particular kind of voyeurism affords, knowing that to see even one fish react to a fly — to see it take, inspect or refuse — is an experience far more intense and gratifying than catching any number of fish blind.

Sight-fishing is a distinctly New Zealand innovation. Not that you won't see fish in the US or Europe, but the nature of our rivers and trout — the almost dizzying clarity of water when you look into it, and the relatively low densities of fish — often make sight-fishing not a choice but a necessity. After all, would a hunter start randomly firing his rifle at the forest hoping to hit a deer he knows is in there somewhere?

Maybe it's because we've both put in a lot of river mileage, flogging the water without seeing the fish first, or perhaps it is a residue of my years as a fishing guide. Watching clients fishing blind can be intolerably boring, which is why we so insist on finding the fish. Spotting makes a guide feel useful and engaged, a part of the adventure. All other alternatives are grim by comparison. Consider the renowned Scottish gillie who was asked what was the single most important skill for a career fishing guide. After scratching his beard in deep thought he replied: 'I'd have to say it'd be the ability to yawn with your mouth shut.'

There wasn't going to be much yawning on the La Fontaine, though it was difficult to keep our own mouths shut, first out of wonder at the numbers of fish, then for other reasons.

A friendly farmer directed us to a 'good spot', and, true enough, we saw several fish rising even before we got out of the truck. We rigged up in haste — long leaders, fine tippets, and again the infallible #16 Parachute Adams as an opening gambit. I took another look at the river. It seemed almost too good to be true: a dream stream with no wind and mayflies coming off the water like some phantasmagoric upward rain. The fish were rising as far as I could see, and I had a good friend to share it all with. What more could you want? The answer became clear as soon as we began to cast.

I spooked my first fish, and David did his, and we blamed it on our over-excitement and the lack of a warm-up. We giggled a bit at our clumsiness, heckling each other about our casting skills. Weren't Mel Krieger's instructional videos our favourite TV soaps? Did I not, at one time, run a successful fly-fishing school in Wanaka? Wasn't David its best *magna cum laude* graduate? No question there, if past performances were anything to go by, we were two champions in top form, capable of accurate, first-cast presentations, with not a hint of drag to be seen. Only the trout, it seemed, did not appreciate such finesse.

By the time we spooked the next few fish we were fully warmed up — too warm, perhaps. With first casts landing bang on the money now, yet still putting the rises out, we went down in tippet and fly size, then up in flies again, ending up with #12 Dad's Favs. Maybe this was the time for the big guns, I suggested, after spotting *Coloburiscus* mayflies fluttering by. Still, no fish, even though we covered more than a dozen.

The champions' egos were getting slightly bruised by now, their mouths harder and harder to keep shut, not so much due to yawning but to jaw-dropping surprise and frustration. It was still early in the season, but these fish were already impossible.

Sure, we could see plenty of them, but even the most delicate
cast was enough to extinguish a rise. One cast was all it took to send
a fish off at a blurring speed. Worse still, the rises would often
recommence behind us as soon as we moved further upstream.

David finally stated the obvious. 'We have to find fish in faster
water. We'll never get them in this slow-moving stuff.' But therein
lay a problem: in fast water we could not see our fish. Though
there was a big barometric high over the entire South Island,
pockets of the West Coast, including Hari Hari, were socked in
with thick inversion-layer clouds pressing down on the landscape
like a solid grey slab. It made for a beautifully moody scene but also
for tough spotting, with or without polaroids.

We stalked as if walking on egg shells, using every bush for
cover. We wore camo gear and even — totally unreasonably — began
to communicate in hushed voices. Yet invariably we saw the fish
too late. Or perhaps the flat, dim light magnified the trout's
senses. Though we worked as a team — a spotter and a caster — the
fish would often vanish almost miraculously in the time it took
to get into a casting position. At which point the spotter, peeking
from behind the clump of flax, would mutter something like: 'Eh,
I'm having trouble seeing 'im', which translated to 'He's seen you
and he's already gone.'

We'd walked upstream for a good ten hours, and all we had to
show for it were a few panicked refusals. Another farmer, riding
an all-weather quad bike, stopped to ask if we'd had any luck, and
I had neither the heart nor a good reason to explain that, when
it came to fly-fishing, I favoured skills over luck. Clearly, on this
particular day, we were lacking both.

'Lot of them jokers *get skunked* here,' the cocky went on,
unperturbed. 'That's the expression you use, in'it?'

Ouch! As if we needed a reminder. I was acutely aware of the
white stripe of a skunk creeping up my spine. At this late hour
in the day it was reaching the last of my thoracic vertebrae. We
desperately needed some sun to improve the odds, but it seemed
that a sunny day on the coast was like rain in Alice Springs — not
impossible, but highly unlikely.

At our turnaround point I sat down on the bank and pulled
a flask of Clynelish out of my vest. Usually, I use it to celebrate,
but now I needed something to lift the spirit. I never thought that
fishing could be so tough. It seemed that the dream river would
have to remain just that — a dream. I took a swig, then glanced
downstream and saw David bracing against his rod as if he was

possum nymph

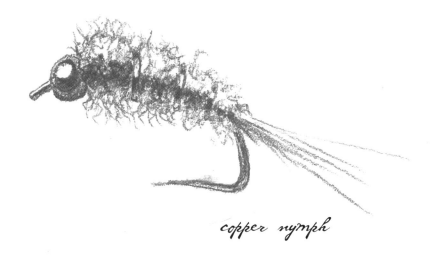

copper nymph

trying to pull the bottom out of the river. Not a snag either. A blurring flash of whisky-gold as a solid fish leaped out of the water was proof enough of that.

It transpired that, never one to brood or despair, David had abandoned our 'See no fish, make no cast' motto and begun casting blind into the first likely riffle. The fish took the big Dad's Fav on the second cast. He landed the fish, released it, and refreshed the fly with a shake-dry. By the time I joined him he was a couple of metres further upstream and hooked up with an even larger fish that was pulling hard for the safety of the sunken willows, but never made it there.

Two fish with three casts, after a day of nothing — it was

> *Two fish with three casts, after a day of nothing — it was something of a shock. After a couple of blind casts into the feed line I had a fish, too, and David was on to his third . . . how good it felt to wash off that skunk.*

something of a shock. After a couple of blind casts into the feed line I had a fish, too, and David was on to his third.

'Too easy,' he said, watching the released fish dart for the deep water. Exactly. How good it felt to wash off that skunk.

It was as if David's breakthrough undid some weather hex that was gripping the valley, for as we woke up in the camper early the next morning the coast was clear, with not a cloud in sight. What a difference this made! Now we could see the fish in fast broken water, and, most of the time, they could not see us. Moreover, they were nymphing voraciously, and we could finally put to the test the secret weapons we'd only recently procured — the new-season bionic 'rubber legs' nymphs tied by guide and fly tier extraordinaire Stu Tripney.

If you want to dramatically increase your catch rate I recommend you study the flies that guides themselves make and use. They are often different from what you can buy in tackle shops — slimmer, more refined and more durable. There is an elegant practicality to these flies, one that comes from hundreds of days on the river and hours at the vice. There are parachutes with orange foam posts for extra buoyancy and visibility, Pheasant Tail nymphs without *any* pheasant in them, generic Cul de Canard (CDC) dries which you can cut down to size on the river to match the hatch — this last one being my own humble contribution to the guides' stash of secrets and tricks.

True enough, Stu's #16 brown 'rubber legs' nymph, the ubiquitous Dad's Fav, and, finally, my Kakahi Queens, too, would

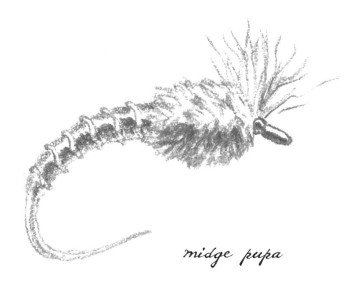

midge pupa

prove the only flies we needed that and all of the next day. We
stalked the banks of the La Fontaine and its tributary, Berry Creek,
finding feeding fish, catching some, missing others, helping each
other to net those we'd managed to fool. With strong overhead
sunlight the balance of odds was more even, and our sight-fishing
rule was in force once again. By lunchtime of the second day
we had stopped counting the fish. The dream river was finally
delivering on its promise.

On the fourth day the slab of clouds returned and we knew
our time was up. There was still plenty more water to explore,
but we'd have to fish it blind and we did not want to dilute the
experience of the past two days. After all, fly-fishing has nothing
to do with numbers and everything to do with magic, and in this
La Fontaine had lived up to its name. It was as hard as it gets, and
just as fabulous.

If you dare to test yourself against it, I wish you Godspeed. Just
be kind on yourself: Pick a sunny day.

November

 'AHV BIN FISHIN' AW MAH LIFE,'
the man said to me on the bank of the Makarora
River and I was tempted to ask: 'And? You ever
caught anything?' I did not say that, of course, not
out loud. After all, the man was paying me to be out here with
him, and besides, right now I could not spare an idle word.
For the umpteenth time I was up to my elbows in the thicket
of riverside matagouri which, if you are not familiar with it,
is a native tree that is all one-inch thorns, and which makes
crumpled coils of barbed wire look and feel positively benign.

The tree was moving violently to the rhythm of the man's
forward casts but he seemed completely oblivious of the fact.

'The damned thing won't go out,' he hollered at his line,
ignoring my shouted pleas to stop casting. Here I had to agree.
The line wasn't going to go out, not without that tree, though to
give the man his credit, he was doing everything in his power to
uproot it.

Several fish — all solid rainbows in crystal-cold mountain water — were rising in our vicinity, taking large terrestrials with the ferocity of punches hitting the surface from underneath. On the Makarora, superbly scenic but not known for large numbers of fish, such a spectacle is relatively rare, and I was hoping to cash in on this good fortune. But from the way my lifelong angler was casting, it looked as if the fish would finish their feed unmolested. Though they'd been feeding for nearly an hour, and we'd been here for just as long, none of the fish had yet seen our fly, much less had a chance to take it.

The offending tree and its neighbours were taking a heavy toll on my supply of tippet material, and several of my Yellow Humpies, deep in the thicket of thorns, looked as if they were spinning themselves fluorocarbon cocoons. I dutifully untangled the line and leader, cutting, retying, all the while allowing for the jerking pulls as my man continued to cast. He was so mesmerised by the rising fish he did not seem to notice or hear anything else, least of all my calls and suggestions. To give my mind a momentary respite I let it drift forward a few hours. That sundowner gin-and-tonic was going to taste really good.

How odd, I thought. I was getting paid a clean dollar a minute to do what I love doing: being on a river, in fresh air and sun, staring into the water for unreasonably long periods of time, trying to catch fish. Yet it all felt like torture. Each of those minutes was sixty full seconds long, and getting through a day like this was akin to measuring time all the way back to the Big Bang.

I had to get away, if only for a moment, to compose myself, do the best I could under the circumstances. I left my man to his antics, ostensibly to scout out the river ahead and find more fish, possibly even bigger fish. I crossed over well below him, then went up the opposite side. A couple of hundred metres upstream, looking down from a high bank, I saw a particularly large rainbow feeding with abandon, taking insects with an audible snap of its jaws, the way a retriever dog snatches a stick out of the water. It was sleek, pristine, achingly beautiful, and catchable with even a half-decent cast.

I looked back at my client, briefly considered bringing him over, knowing too well that he probably wouldn't be able to get across the river without dunking us both in the drink, concluding that in all fairness, with the skills and attitude he brought to our outing, he did not deserve to catch this fish.

I also thought that this was a terrible attitude for a professional guide to have, and this conclusion was final and

To a riverside aesthete like me the world of pounds and inches multiplied by the number of fish caught was foreign. I had made a bad career choice, like a vegetarian trying to be a butcher.

life-changing. I had to quit. To a riverside aesthete like me the world of pounds and inches multiplied by the number of fish caught was foreign. I had made a bad career choice, like a vegetarian trying to be a butcher.

By that time I had worked as a guide for several seasons, developing a growing clientele and generating enough turnover to make guiding a full-time job if I wanted to. In the process I had spent a good many days in the company of usually affluent people from around the world. I'd done a good job, or so they told me, and my clients had been almost without exception agreeable and friendly people. But it seemed as if we fished for entirely different reasons.

They usually arrived decked out head to toe in the most expensive fishing attire you could find, clutching the finest equipment, hyped up on brochures and magazine advertorials about New Zealand's plentiful trophy trout. I watched them and thought 'so far, so good'.

But when you turn your passion into a business, begin peddling the very thing you cherish, it's like sending your loved one into a ring for a prize fight — she's bound to take a few hits. She might lose, even get knocked out. Mine was often decked, groggily listening to the KO countdown.

The punches usually started coming as soon as we got to a river. My enthusiastic clients rarely had the skills or the stamina to pursue their desires (think of a hunter who cannot shoot). Worse, many considered trout not the beautiful, wild, free creatures I hold so precious, but mere playthings to be toyed with, a commodity to be acquired, weighed and counted.

With a few notable exceptions, these would-be fishermen were so far removed from the natural world it was as if they considered their sport a swipe-your-credit-card-to-begin virtual-reality game. Often they weren't fit enough to negotiate a stony riverbed, yet their expectations were as huge as their impatience to fulfil them. To me, they seemed to have lost their footing on Earth and gone adrift in the dreamland of sound bites, digitalised reality and instant gratification.

Well, fly-fishing isn't like that, not in New Zealand anyway. You need to be a hunter, not a shopper. You have to go humbly and quietly, crawl on your knees if need be, respect your quarry. For many, coming down to such an earth-bound reality was a crash landing, and I was the ambulance man helping them back onto their feet. If I had more patience and took it all less seriously, or perhaps if there was a drive-in river full of farmed trophy fish, I'd be a rich and satisfied man. Or maybe just rich. As it was, frustration became the *plat du jour*, served all day, often several days in a row. My passion for trout began to grow cold.

Then, one day, shortly after the Makarora experience, another client presented me with a gift, the memoir of an American fishing guide, Dave Ames. The book was entitled *A Good Life Wasted*. It was an average read, but it was the title that I found most arresting. The message could not have been clearer. I took the hint, and the following day I shut down shop, taking my website offline, farming out all my bookings to other guides. The next day my joy of fishing returned like a long-lost friend.

Still, I have always taken every opportunity to fish with other guides. They are — the good ones, at least, for there are all kinds — exceptionally amiable companions and skilful anglers. They have to be, because the job calls for being both a baby-sitter and a magician, with huge emphasis on the latter. Good guides are used to fishing in all weather and water conditions, and against all odds.

When the fishing is tough, when all hope is waning and it feels like you are never going to catch another fish, they always have a trick or two up their sleeves for just such a moment, a secret 'honey hole' place or technique, which is why I've come to think of them as magicians conjuring not so much rabbits out of hats as trout out of water.

Above all, guides are an unending source of first-hand knowledge, a proxy for learning and understanding the mysteries of trout. And isn't that what fly-fishing is about?

'My *Rhyacophila* is a bit big,' Smiley confided to me over a coffee on the bank of the Clutha. His expression was both disdainful and worried, leaving no doubt that the issue was a serious one. Was there a yarn shop in town, he wanted to know.

Around the world, stock markets were going crazy, first yo-yoing to the tune of economic news, then simply freefalling so that their graphs resembled mammoth ski jumps with no spring step at the bottom. Smiley should have been worried about that, since the family nest egg was placed in the shares of a certain petroleum company, and they were probably devaluing right now like some Central American peso. Instead, he fussed about the size of his *Rhyacophila*.

The day before, Smiley had caught a nymphing trout in the Clutha, just across the river from where we were now, and as he was unhooking it the fish disgorged a mouthful of caddis nymphs, green and tiny. To a less educated eye, that's what they would have remained — green and tiny bugs — but to Smiley they were clearly the *Rhyacophila* caddis, larvae of an industrious little critter which not only swim free in the river (unlike most bottom-dwelling nymphs), but also snare their own prey with microscopic nets, ingenious but invisible without a magnifying glass.

In his van, in a vice clamped to the steering wheel, Smiley promptly tied several imitations, but, lacking the correct materials, he made them too big and clunky. Now it bugged him, so to speak, that the flies not only looked ugly, but they weren't catching any fish either. After thirty-one years of guiding out of Jackson Hole, Wyoming, and sixty years on the planet, Smiley had his priorities down pat. The financial markets would do what they would do; he could not help any of that. But while the season was young and the trout hungry, getting those damned *Rhyacophila* nymphs right was critical.

Besides, unlike the rescue of the global economy, long overreaching and now frantically trying to back-paddle, Smiley's particular problem was eminently solvable, the solution to it simple and inexpensive. All it required was a tuft of fine green dubbing and a happy hour at the vice. In a world going crazy by the day, such a task offered a modicum of sanity.

I told him I was a *Rhyacophila* fan myself, and that in my travel fly-tying kit I had just the right kind of green fluff for the job at hand. Smiley's face lit up as if he'd just heard some crackling good news from his stock broker. He'd have some of that green fluff this very moment, if that was all right by me.

For several years now, after guiding six and seven days a week on rivers around the Grand Teton and Yellowstone, Smiley has been spending his off seasons in New Zealand, flying his paraglider when the weather was perfect, fly-fishing when it was less so, playing golf when the wind got up too strong, reading paperback novels in his van when all other options failed.

I was still guiding when he came by to introduce himself and to talk shop, and I took an instant liking to him and his minimalist approach. He wore a uniform of fast-drying zip-off pants and a matching shirt, and his glasses, thick and round, were permanently wired to his studious face with a keeper strap, turning into dark polaroids whenever there was enough sunlight. For six months of the year he lived in his Toyota Town Ace — no salon on wheels by any stretch of imagination — into which he managed to pack all the mod cons for which most folks I know need an entire holiday house. Apart from Smiley himself, in the van lived his paraglider — the size of a backpack you would take for a three-week trip in the bush — a golf bag with a good selection of baffies and mashie-niblicks, a crate of fishing gear, a small library of paperbacks and all the living and cooking essentials. He even had running water, courtesy of refilled bladders from empty three-litre wine casks.

I was just packing my own camper for a few days on the Tekapo River, and I asked Smiley if he'd care to join me. The 'take' was instantaneous, and the following day we were driving north in a convoy, up and over the Lindis Pass.

Ever since I first fished the Tekapo a decade or so ago, it has become a regular annual entry in my fly-fishing calendar, usually around mid-November or early December, sometimes in April as well. Smiley, it turned out, knew the river well, too, but from a different side. His van — he called it his 'Town Ass' — was a 2WD, with delicate-looking tyres, low clearance and a dislike for roads that were unsealed and corrugated. As most of the roads around the Tekapo River are 4WD tracks ploughed through rough riverbeds, Smiley was limited to the shores of Lake Benmore and the lower part of the Tekapo River, accessible from there on foot.

'Some of the best fishing I've ever had,' he said, and, considering his river mileage, this meant a whole lot more than if anyone else had said it. 'The lower river has plenty of fish, and the lakeshore, man, it's like bonefish flats only with trout.' He concluded with a tally of numbers multiplied by inches and pounds. It all sounded terribly impressive.

At its dammed outlet at the bottom of Lake Tekapo, the river looks dead, turned off at the source, its bed dried up and forlorn, a victim of progress and a sacrifice to civilisation. But follow its bouldery course downstream and you realise it is not so easy to kill a river. Only a few kilometres below the dam the Tekapo begins to flow again, gathering itself from underground seepage and feeder streams, twisting through the leather-brown desert of the Mackenzie Country, a vein of greenery and life, and full of trout.

The fish here, browns and rainbows, are not only plentiful but also relatively easy to catch, and this, over the past few years, has given the river a rather unhealthy popularity. When I fished it the previous year, perhaps a little too early in the season, there were 4WDs staking out every good pool. The place looked more like a mid-week Tongariro than anything in the South Island. Still, I've always fished the Tekapo for more than its trout. It is a place to go with a dog and to let her roam free, safe from cars and poisons, and get herself so happily exhausted chasing rabbits and hares that she curls up at your feet to sleep every time you stop to cast to a fish or change flies. A place to make campfires of bone-dry driftwood and, when they go out, to watch Pleiades and Orion rise and rotate overhead.

The night sky over Mackenzie is uncommonly clear and bright, and the Milky Way looks like a splash of glitter paint stretching from one horizon to the other. The stars are so sharp and numerous they seem almost fake, like the background for a George Lucas movie.

For this reason, the Mackenzie Country has attracted astronomers for as long as it has fly-fishermen. The astronomers have set up a permanent camp on top of an island-like mountain called Mt John, dotting its bold summit with the white domes of six telescopes, which sprout from the tawny tussock like giant puffballs. Recently, the same astronomers proposed that the night sky of the Mackenzie be declared the Earth's first Starlight Reserve, a kind of World Heritage Park in the sky. It was from the summit of Mt John, where the big eye of a 1.8-metre telescope scans the sky on every clear night, that the existence of an entire solar system similar to our own was confirmed in the constellation of Sagittarius. I had followed the news with interest, since the Archer, a straight shooter, as I like to think of him, is also my own Zodiac sign, but so far there has been no word from the scientists as to whether the new planetary system has any worthwhile trout waters.

Smiley and I parked near the Twizel River outlet, rigged up and tramped over to the Tekapo. By the time we began to fish it was already midday, and I worried that this piece of river would surely have been already fished. But Smiley was unfazed. I did not yet know that one of his key professional abilities was finding pockets of good water that had been missed or ignored by other anglers.

'In the States, you never hope to have a piece of river to yourself,' he said. 'If you get enough room to cast you consider yourself lucky.'

I found that hard to believe.

'Man, when the box canyon section of the Snake opens in Harriman State Park, there will be 300 people spread out over two miles of the river.'

Well, I thought, maybe Tekapo wasn't getting crowded after all.

It was good to be back. For most of the year the land here is parched brown by the sun and the hot nor'westerly winds that sweep down from the mountains, the grass so desiccated it crunches underfoot. But in spring and early summer, flowering lupins add splotches of white, purple and blue, and an explosion of Californian poppies covers the grey river gravels like orange confetti. This day, too, was fabulous, with the sun beating down, the white pyramid of Mt Cook glittering over the northern horizon, the fish so plentiful and eager it seemed we could do no wrong.

I knew we were on to a good thing when I spied a fish in a pool's tailout. I thought it was shallow enough to try it with a dry, and cast a chunky Royal Wulff. We watched the fish rise and follow the fly for a good two metres before it turned back upstream and returned to its station without a take. I changed to an Elk Hair Caddis, and this time the fish did not hesitate. The next one was Smiley's, but it refused his nymphs and continued to cruise down the eye of the pool.

'He's coming towards you,' Smiley called out, pulling in his line to retie.

'You mind?' I asked, feeling on a roll.

'Not at all, go for it.'

The fish was clearly visible now over the light sandy bottom, followed closely by the twin of its shadow which seemed as solid and sharply defined as the trout itself. Down on my knees, I let the current straighten the line downstream, afraid that even a single false cast could spook the fish. Then, pulling the line off the water, letting the drag against the surface power the cast, I plopped the fly two metres in front of the trout and waited.

For a moment the fish agitated, and I expected him to dart off into the deep, but then, with a burst of speed that left a jet trail of churned-out silt in its wake, the trout charged forward and snatched the fly. The fish's agitation was clearly its excitement at the sight of prey. I could well relate to that.

When the initial zigzags of the trout subsided, turning into a tug of war of strength and wills, I related to Smiley the two critical bits of information: the name of the fly and its size.

'Elk Hair it is then,' he said, tying one on. But as it is often the case with trout, no other fish that day would take the caddis.

Not that we cared what they were taking, for there seemed to be no end to fish in just a couple of pools. Our small nymphs, 16s and 18s, seemed irresistible to them and the fish took the flies with such ferocity that they dunked the yarn indicators, so there was never any doubt what was happening down under water.

On the way back to the camp, in ponds fed by a tiny spring creek, we saw two more fish and caught them, too, though both came off our barbless hooks on the jump. Smiley shook his head. 'You know, for most of my clients back in the States, *any* of the fish we caught today would have been the fish of the lifetime,' he said. 'And we got how many? Ten? A dozen?'

I said I didn't know; I hadn't counted them, though the idea of a dozen lifetimes in one afternoon seemed just about right. I thought of Henry Spencer, and wished he could be here with us. How much more keenly he would appreciate those extra lifetimes than either of us did.

We were ready for more of the same the following day, bigger and more intense, and hopefully even more numerous, and indeed the morning promised just that — cloudless blue and perfect for spotting, still and warm and full of untold potential. Being the early birds this time, we even had an untouched beat. But what on earth had happened to the fish?

From the first cast they refused everything we offered them — nymphs and dries, big and small. They never spooked, but seemed uninterested in food, many of them swimming slowly downstream in an almost melancholy mood, if such a thing can be said of fish.

We could see plenty of trout, all right. On one clear gravel shelf sloping into a riffle Smiley pointed out no less than eight distinct dark shapes, and he left them for me and moved upstream, assuming I'd pick them off one by one, cleaning up the pool.

It was a perfect water for a large dry fly — shallow, broken and fast — and the shapes of trout seemed to shimmer just under its surface. I tied on a buoyant Wulff and cast it to the bottommost fish. Instantly, the trout rose with a splash, its head breaking the surface, and I struck, sure I had him. But as the line tore free from the water the sucking noise and slash it made next to the fish caused the trout to turn downstream and streak for the deep water.

The same thing happened on the next fish, then the next. In this kind of water it was impossible to tell if the fish took the fly or just followed but refused it, and so I had to strike each time, and each time the fish spooked. I changed flies, going through a Humpy, a caddis, then a small Parachute mayfly, but the results were always the same. By the time I finished I could see no more dark shapes on the gravel shelf. I had indeed cleaned up the pool.

I walked up to rejoin Smiley, feeling asinine and dejected, ready to commiserate on the downturn of our fortunes, when I saw that he was just about to land a fish and was slipping a holey piece of tan-brown stocking over the palm of his hand so that he could tail his catch. (Smiley believes this type of landing is kinder on the fish than netting it, and I have come to share this view, at least with smaller fish.)

It turned out this wasn't his first fish, either. Apparently, he figured out this particular trout malaise and took countermeasures. He could not see them, but his white-yarn indicator was dipping down into the dark pool with satisfying regularity.

'The water temperature's way up,' he said. 'You gotta fish deep and small. That's where they're eatin'.' To prove his words he produced a thermometer out of a slit in his vest. It was a long steel probe, like a sharpened bicycle spoke, with a head the size of a ten-inch nail which housed the dial. He dipped the electrode in the river and waited the prescribed few seconds.

'See,' he said, checking the dial. 'Almost 65°F [18°C]. For trout, that's just short of boiling.'

I have seen both guides and other anglers dipping their digital thermometers in trout waters, feigning shock and disdain at the readouts, shaking their heads in consternation. Frankly, it always seemed to me a complicated and self-aggrandising way to explain or justify why they were not catching anything. But now Smiley was using it to the opposite effect: we were not catching fish, and he took a temperature reading and this gave him a clue, an understanding to how to solve our particular problem. I was intrigued, because unlike all previous thermal braggadocios, Smiley's reasoning was as simple and clear as it was practical.

'Fish are cold-blooded creatures, that's what it all comes down to,' he said. 'They have this temperature range in which they're happiest and most active. That'd be around 13.8–14.4°C with four degrees on either side. They start feeding at around 11°C and stop at 19°C. Outside of that, the fish are not interested in much of anything, just trying to get warm or stay cool, getting enough oxygen to breathe.'

Ita's Bionic
Green Beetle

Green Beetle

He reclaimed his thermometer and pocketed it. 'If nothing else, the water temperature gives you a good idea how active the fish are going to be.'

What about the flies, I wanted to know. Were the mayflies and caddises hatching at particular temperatures? Could the thermometer be of any use in anticipating, if not quite predicting, an imminent hatch?

'I don't know about that,' Smiley said, 'In my experience, bugs hatch when they're good and ready. Besides, you probably don't want to figure and measure it all up to the last detail. Gotta leave some room for the unexpected.'

For the rest of the afternoon the heat poured down from the sky, on to us, the land and the water. The following day we again tried to fish, but the trout were even more lethargic and disinterested. In the end we drove back to Wanaka and found a cold feeder stream of the Matukituki River.

Smiley took the temperature, and the dial sprang to the ideal 13.3°C. Against an undercut bank we spotted several rainbows holding in the current, jostling for position, and as soon as Smiley cast the indicator dipped and the water exploded as if someone had thrown a brick into it.

The fight quickly shifted downstream, but I stayed on to see if the other fish were still there. From down below I heard Smiley shout.

'Huh! He took the *Rhyacophila*.'

'One small step . . .' I thought. It seemed we had both understood fragments of the larger reality of trout, me about the temperatures and Smiley about his *Rhyacophila*. The world was once again in order and making sense. At least Smiley's world did. Mine was about to be turned inside out.

That November, when I got back home from a magazine assignment, I found that I no longer had a home to come back to. The house was still there, with all its small luxuries and trappings of habit and comfort, but it was now just an empty shell. The woman with whom I had shared it, along with a large and important chunk of my life, had left, and in a way that overshadowed everything we had up to that moment, a lot of which was good.

I guess, after years of silent but insidious erosion, I should have seen it coming, though the reasons for what happened had nothing to do with fishing or spending too much time away, or any other 'my wife told me if I ever go fishing again she'll leave me; I'll surely miss the old gal' type of scenarios on which the statement T-shirt industry thrives. And maybe I did see it coming, but somehow I also hoped that when the inevitable came it would be civil and respectful, a parting of two friends who have travelled together thus far but now reached a fork in the road.

The break-up, the suddenness and sadness of it, had pulled the ground from under my feet, and as with other times of calamity — the death of a friend, or 9/11 — I turned to the river, not so much to fish as to find solace, to be reminded, reassured perhaps, that life goes on, that like a flood of debris or a spill of poison this too shall pass as surely as the rivers flow.

I once lived in the Swiss Alps, where I came across the idea of *hausberg*, or the 'home mountain'. Local tradition has it that each person needs a mountain with which he or she has a particularly deep and personal affinity. It needn't be anything spectacular, a Matterhorn or Eiger. A simple hill will do. What matters is the strength of connection. A *hausberg* is a hideaway where you may have played as a child, and where later you seek solitude during life's tempests. A place to share with your loved ones and only the closest of friends. A landmark which springs to mind when you think of home; the epicentre of your personal heartland. Although I used to climb mountains, and still like to ski off them, and though mountains abound near where I live, I've always favoured the idea of not so much a home mountain as a home river.

Now, watching the Clutha move by with its unceasing vitality,

> *What power and weight simple words can carry. 'I do' and 'I did' can bracket an entire lifetime, one bringing hope and joy at the birth of something new and beautiful, the other a death sentence, the finality of a guillotine.*

always fresh, always new — and feeling the exact opposite of that — I thought of the power of words, how we abuse and misuse them, and how in times like this their original meaning often becomes clear and true. What power and weight simple words can carry. 'I do' and 'I did' can bracket an entire lifetime, one bringing hope and joy at the birth of something new and beautiful, the other a death sentence, the finality of a guillotine.

I again thought of Henry Spencer and a rare glimpse into his private life that he had once offered. He told me how he had sat in a hard hospital chair holding his wife's hand until the end, how he felt the life go out of her, and clawed at it to make it stay, and how it slipped out of his clenched fists. He had grieved for her to the point of insanity and scattered her ashes into a river whose name meant nothing to me but a whole lot to them both. He told me that until then he did not know you could get dehydrated through the shedding of tears, but that, in times like this, it was a real danger.

I thought how sad yet noble and beautiful this all was, how touchingly human, and how cheap and undistinguishing my own story felt by comparison. Yet the river was there for us both, welcoming and compassionate, and now walking its banks, with only the dog for company, I felt a strange sense of kinship with all those who had come here for similar reasons. The words from a song by Francis Cabrel, '*La cabane du pêcheur*' (The fisherman's cabin) came to me unbidden. They translate roughly into something like this:

> If you're crying for your lost love,
> you won't be the last one,

Look well at the fish,
they are often more affectionate.
Go travel a little,
Breathe in the big world.
Afterwards I'll tell you about love
If I can still remember a little.

On the bank of my home river I wept tears of grief I had not
known before. They were, I now realise, not for the real person,
but for the loss of a dream and of innocence. Heraclitus wrote that
you cannot step twice into the same river, though it is equally true
that, coming back to a river, we are never the same, either. Each
time we come to a river, no matter how well we think we know it,
it's as if we are meeting for the first time.

I found a deep swimming hole, stripped down and sat neck-
deep in cold slow-moving water, dunking my head under every
so often until I was so numb from cold I could not feel anything
at all. Mops, my Airedale, a strong but reluctant swimmer, stood
guard over me, square on her haunches right on the water's edge.
Every time I disappeared under the surface she leaped up in
agitation and paced up and down the waterline at a trot. When
I resurfaced she greeted me with barks and tail wags as if we had
not seen each other for days, as if I were returning from some
netherworld, which I guess was not that far from the truth.

Whether the river washed away the pain or just numbed it I'm
not sure, but in the days that followed it was the only thing that
helped, so I repeated it religiously, towelling off hard each time I
came out of the water I until my skin ached with life again.

I knew I was coming around when a close friend who'd been
nursing me through these troubled times read me a line from an
obscure poem which said:

'*From the ashes the phoenix shall rise again, reborn and resplendent.*'

And I thought: did she say a rise? What kind?

Emerger? Caddis? Cicada?

One morning, while refilling the dog's water bowl, I saw the
season's first manuka beetle, drowned but still suspended in the
surface film of the water. It was metallic green, iridescent and
bright as a sequin.

Summer was coming.

December

HAVE YOU EVER CONSIDERED WHAT A miracle it is that we have trout in New Zealand? We don't give it much thought these days, taking it for granted that we can pick up a rod and walk or drive to the nearest river and find a 3, 4 or 5-lb trout rising to passing dries, hoovering nymphs in current troughs, chasing bullies or smelt. But think about this: for scores of anglers from the countries our trout come from, a visit to New Zealand is a lifetime dream, a pilgrimage. They would much rather come here — and many do — than to fish for trout in their native waters. Isn't that in itself a wonder of wonders?

In a country where the arrival of other exotic animals — rabbits, stoats and deer — has been synonymous with environmental disaster, the introduction of trout seems a remarkable story of success. To be sure, being the top-of-the-food-chain predator, the fish have decimated many species of native aquatic fauna, and eco-purists consider it something of a freshwater possum, a noxious pest. But we forgive them — the eco-purists, that is — their noble but misguided point of view. After all, following their logic and desires of restoring the land to what it once was, before the arrival of humans and our entourage of pests, we would all have to leave these beautiful islands, too. It stands to reason, and there is evidence wherever you look, that of all species introduced to this island paradise *Homo sapiens* has been the greatest pest of all.

When it comes to trout, at least in popular retrospect, the settlers improving on God are not seen as those raising ecological hell. In the late nineteenth century they said: 'Let there be trout in New Zealand' — truly outstanding trout, they might well have added — and it was so, and it was good.

The reality of this creation was not so straightforward, however, for in the piscatorial history of this country trout were an afterthought, almost an accident. At first, all the attention was on Atlantic salmon.

In the days before refrigeration trucks and ice-cream vans, an ingenious Australian named James Youl devised wooden packaging crates, complete with a sprinkler system, which, when enclosed inside an ice-house, would keep salmon eggs below 9°C, thus retarding their hatching for up to 140 days, long enough to withstand an arduous ocean journey to the colonies.

Bob McDowall, New Zealand's eminent ichthyologist, now retired from the National Institute of Water and Atmospheric Research, described the procedure: 'The salmon ova were packed into small wooden boxes with perforated tops, bottoms and sides. In each box were placed layers of charcoal, then of ice, carefully washed moss, and then the ova, which were covered with more moss and ice, before the top was attached. The total consignment comprised 189 boxes, which were stacked into the ice house and covered to a height of nearly three metres with ice.' The whole contraption weighed 56 tonnes. It arrived in Australia in 1863, after eighty-four days at sea. Only 30,000 eggs were still alive, and from those 700 salmon hatched.

That experiment in shipping was the beginning of the importation of Atlantic salmon to New Zealand which, according to McDowall, was to be 'the most enduring and intensive effort anywhere in the world to introduce an exotic species into a new country'. Let's add that this century-long saga was also a monumental failure. For reasons still unknown, the fish did not take to our waters, though McDowall speculates that the transfer of the fish from one hemisphere to another may have caused their internal compass to malfunction, so that they simply went out to sea and never found their way back.

Between 1864 and 1910 alone, there were twenty-four shipments of Atlantic salmon, totalling five million ova, but save for small populations of landlocked and dwarfed fish persisting in Lakes Te Anau, Manapouri, Gunn and Fergus, no evidence exists that the sea-run salmon ever returned to New Zealand rivers. On the other hand, the success of brown and later rainbow trout exceeded all expectations, though, admittedly, the beginnings were equally shaky.

In 1864, the ship *Norfolk* sailed from England to Tasmania, carrying 118,000 ova of Atlantic salmon, plus a small bonus package of brown trout supplied by two English salmophiles: Frank Buckland, who contributed a thousand eggs of stream browns from Itchen River, near Winchester, and Francis Francis, who added 1500 eggs of sea-run trout from Wey and Wycombe Rivers.

From this stock, three years later, the Tasmanian Royal Society donated 800 ova to the Acclimatisation Society in Christchurch, and 400 to the branch in Otago. But the passage across the Tasman was long and rough, and the eggs arrived in poor condition. None of the Otago ova hatched, and the Christchurch shipment produced only three fish.

As if that wasn't bad enough, a freak overnight rain storm flooded the Hagley Park hatchery, and the three fish escaped into the Avon River. A major fish hunt ensued, and two of the escapees were recaptured, luckily a male and a female. They were reared to maturity and spawned successfully. In the country that has become known as the anglers' paradise, these were our salmonid Adam and Eve.

Some chroniclers discredit the story today, and certainly this scenario of creation does not mention the countless volunteers who laboured for many years to create New Zealand's trout fishery. An 1868 Otago shipment — 800 eggs brought in by Charles Clifford, of which 720 hatched in Opoho hatchery and were released all over Otago and Southland — was but an encouraging beginning. In the wake of such successes, hatcheries mushroomed all around the country, pouring out millions of trout fry and fingerlings. Between 1869 and 1923, the Otago Acclimatisation Society alone released twenty-three million trout in its district, and there were over twenty other societies around the country.

Not all introductions 'took'. An effort to introduce mackinaw — a lake char widely distributed in North America, where it can

grow up to 45 kg — ended rather abruptly near Arthur's Pass. The
transport of fish customarily happened in the cool of the night,
but the tanker filled with mackinaw fingerlings destined for Lake
Kaniere near Hokitika was delayed on its transalpine crossing, and
as the sun rose, so did the temperature of the cistern. Faced with
the imminent death of his cargo, the driver aborted the journey
and released the fish into the first handy stretch of water, which
happened to be lakes Pearson and Grasmere. A small population
still lingers in the former, but the lake is too shallow and too warm
for the fish to thrive, so they average only around 1.5 lb. They
remain the only stock of mackinaw in New Zealand.

There is no biological limit to how large a trout can grow, for
their size is determined only by availability of suitable habitat
and food supply. In New Zealand, the first was ideal, the second
abundant, and so the newly introduced fish quickly grew to
extraordinary sizes, and the ensuing trout fever was as intense as
any gold rush.

Hamish Furneaux, a retired pharmacist in Wanaka, a collector
of trout literature and a lifelong angler, once told me about his
childhood in Manawatu: 'It was a truly remarkable time. Men
like my father would keep their rods in the cow shed, and in the
evening, after milking, walk across the paddocks to the river, and
easily catch enough trout to feed the whole family. In the Old
Country, this was simply unthinkable.'

What was also unthinkable was how huge New Zealand trout
grew. Early reports reaching England met with incredulity. What
could the British angling establishment make of news that their
beloved and lordly trout grew so large they could not be caught on
a fly; that, as in the case of two Lake Heron 34-lb browns in 1884,
they had to be either shot or harpooned like a whale?

The stories kept on coming. In 1927, spinning off a
Queenstown beach in Lake Wakatipu, a Dunedin dentist named
Boot caught a brown trout that weighed close to 17 kg. A similar-
sized rainbow was winched out of the Mangamutu Stream near
Taupo, and in the lake itself, one night in 1925, a certain J.D.A.
Painton caught eleven fish, ten of which were over 9 kg. At the same
time, Rotorua anglers customarily released any fish under 5 kg.

Although Bryn Hammond, author of the highly readable *New
Zealand Encyclopaedia of Fly Fishing*, writes that the giants of that era are
gone forever, the lunker trout are still undoubtedly out there, and
not only under the Mackenzie Country salmon-farm cages. Over
a decade ago, a Kaikoura helicopter pilot, Noel Boyd, found one
such trophy. He was working on deer recovery in the mountains

In 1927, spinning off a Queenstown beach in Lake Wakatipu, a Dunedin dentist named Boot caught a brown trout that weighed close to 17 kg. A similar-sized rainbow was winched out of the Mangamutu Stream near Taupo . . .

above Molesworth Station, when, from the air, he saw it floating on the surface on Lake McRae. He landed nearby and recovered the trout, which had been dead for some time. The fish weighed 15 kg and is now on display in a Nelson airport hangar, procured, you might say, with an imitation of a dragonfly: a helicopter.

If November rolled by with equinoctial gales and infrequent windows of settled weather, December arrived with a reprise of winter — frost and snow down to ground level, and wind so cold it seemed to blow straight from the Antarctic. As I looked out the window, the notion of the imminent global warming seemed like a practical joke.

I stayed home and worked, and thought of those large trout. Most anglers admire large fish, but it has always mystified me how for many of them the essence of a day's fishing could be reduced to poundage, a mathematical calculation of the numbers of fish caught and their weight — as if fishing were some sort of extraction industry where you were appraised, evaluated, even vindicated by the weight of what you pulled out of the river. Poundage is also supposed to be a quantifier of skills, somehow inexplicably making a guy whose fish weighed in at 6¾ lb a better angler — indeed, a superior human being — than the next guy whose fish pulled the scales to a mere 6½. And God forbid if the first guy caught another fish, even a humble 5-pounder. His tally would be then 11¾ lb, making him a clear winner, a trout hero to be reckoned with, an expert whose liberally given advice should be considered priceless.

If you could pluck hackles from such a strutting rooster, the dry
flies made from them would be like miniature *Titanics*, unsinkable
until the moment of truth.

Sure, there is a certain minimum weight or size above which
the fish actually feels like a fish you've caught and not like bait you
put on to catch something with. In New Zealand, lucky folks that
we are, I'd put this at around 2 lb, though in many less fortunate
countries this would be already regarded as something of a trophy.
Beyond that, the big-fish fanfaronade always seemed to me like
some aspiring alpha male pep talk.

I, for one, consider myself free from what Bryn Hammond
calls the 'tyranny of the avoirdupois'. Maybe there was a place and
reason for it in some distant past, when we were still hunter-
gatherers, but nowadays the fact that you're catching more or
bigger fish than other anglers is not going to do much for your
rank and status in the general populace, least of all among the
females, alpha or otherwise.

If you have fished long enough, you have probably noticed that
good anglers, and I mean *really* good anglers, rarely brag about
their catch, unless they are guides, in which case it's usually an
exercise in marketing and self-promotion. Such anglers, in fact,
often downplay fish tallies, not so much from some false sense
of modesty but to protect the particular river and the quality of
experience they found there. When you ask them how they got on,
and they reply, 'Ah, only got a couple,' all the while avoiding eye
contact and further elaboration, there is an excellent chance that
the fishing was good, maybe even exceptionally so, and the 'couple'
was more likely a dozen, and good ones, too.

Over the years I have experienced thirty-plus fish days, and
zero fish days, and many scenarios in-between, and I've found
that more fish does not always add up to a better day. Nor is size
a deciding factor. Some of the big fish I've caught, such as the
double-figure rainbow in the Otamangakau canal near Turangi,
which fought with about as much spirit as a sunken brick, are
memorable precisely because, against great expectations, they
were so ordinary, uneventful even. On the contrary, a spring-
creek 4-pounder, which took a tiny dry and led me on a merry-
go-round bush bash up and down the bank, and finally made me
jump in and fill my waders with what felt less like water and more
like liquid ice, is sure to remain my all-time trophy. Maybe that's
why I have not been back to the Turangi canals, while I haunt every
spring creek I can find with the eagerness of a bloodhound on a
game trail.

No-name damsel nymph

Then there are those rarest of moments when the fish is both big and memorable. One of them gave me the most bizarre fishing experience I've ever had.

It was on the Inangahua River below Reefton, in the days when I was happy to blind-cast into every bit of likely water, hoping, and with good reason, that if I did that often enough something would eventually come out and eat one of my flies. I was about to finish this long and fishless day when, at my designated turnaround pool, a large trout rose and took my dry fly. At the time, not knowing much else, I fished with an 8 lb Maxima tippet all the way through, using a fat and buoyant Royal Wulff dry for an indicator and a generic beadhead nymph underneath.

The fish porpoised in the white water, then vanished back into it, but when I struck I felt both heft and anger. A lot of anger. The next forty or so minutes were a blur, a give-and-take (but mostly give) tug of war which took us a kilometre downstream, sent me tripping over bone-white boulders, running away from the river's edge to keep up the tension, losing all the gains again, running, running down, shaking the cramps out of my forearms.

The fish would not give up, and we were fast approaching a bridge with its pylons and deep channels in-between, each a palisade of flood-borne tree debris, all of it spelling multiple options for escape. It looked as if the fish had won, but just then it

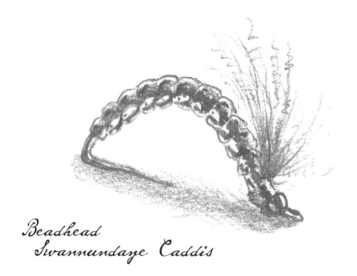

*Beadhead
Swannundaze Caddis*

relented, and, Maxima being thick but unbreakable, I dragged the
trout into the shallows and held it there. We were both spent, but
with the line still twanging like a guitar string, I netted the monster.

Those days I still carried a net with built-in scales and, okay,
let's have it, the fish clocked in at just under 9 lbs. I went to
unhook it and instantly saw the cause of this hellish combat. The
trout was foul-hooked, right in the cartilage-hard flesh between its
pectoral fins. It had obviously come for the dry, as I saw, but it did
not take it. Thinking that it had, I struck and hooked it with the
nymph, which imbedded itself deep and held fast.

I took it out with my forceps, pulled out the fly and the point
of the hook left a tiny red pinprick on the fish's skin. Then I saw
something else: next to it were two more identical marks, roughly
forming a triangle no bigger than a ten cent coin. The fish had
been caught, in exactly the same manner, twice before, and
recently. It must be tough to be a big trout on a popular river.

I started rethinking my ideas on pounds and sizes when I met
'Fiordland Fred'. A mutual friend put us in touch with each other,
anticipating that with all we had in common we'd make instant
riverside buddies. We met on the equivalent of a blind date on our
favourite river in Southland.

I emailed 'Fred' directions to my moderately secret camp spot
on the river, and he knew exactly where it was, which I took for a
good omen. Then, as we met in the evening, I had a nauseating
pang of doubt. Within a couple of sentences of introducing
himself, 'Fred' told me that he was only really interested in big
fish. He was a collector of *doubles*, with anything short of 10 lb
barely worth a cast. Well, maybe not quite. Nines were okay, eights

were fine, but anything smaller did not really count. Though it was only early December, he'd already got a few this season, at which point he gave me a recital of memorised diary entries: days, numbers, poundage, the usual.

I idly wondered if perhaps his sex life was all it could have been, whether there was some small genetic problem, a shortcoming of sorts. I took a sip of wine and thought: 'Man, have I just signed up for two days of "mine is bigger than yours" rhetoric?'

Things are often not what they appear to be, and my first impression of Fred could not have been more wrong. He was courteous to a fault, spotted fish with ease, then, inexplicably, offered them all to me. I felt I was being guided on a river I've come to favour almost more than any other. The fishing was hard, with the trout either so flighty you could spook them just by blinking or so unresponsive that nothing short of prodding with the rod tip would make them move away.

Still, by lunchtime we had four fish, with one confidently taking a small Blue Dun mayfly in water dappled with sunlight and the strong shadows of the beech trees. For me that fish was an epiphany of purism: one cast, a take without a hint of hesitation, not so much a strike but the gentlest lift of the rod, a spirited combat with glorious aerobatics, a definite keeper as the memories of the season would go.

All the fish were mine, too, because for a reason of his own Fred gallantly abdicated each of his turns so that I had almost all the opportunities. He was happy to walk and watch me fish, he said; he had absolutely no problem with that.

His strategically concealed and only mildly ulterior motive became apparent as the day progressed. He was accumulating credits, so that when he wanted to fish there would be absolutely no question that it was finally his turn. It transpired that Fred had walked the river two weeks earlier, and in one of its upper pools had spied a particularly large fish. It was not quite a double, but near enough to make him want to walk all day and give up all other opportunities for a shot at the big one.

This, I must say, intrigued me. It was clearly not an ego trip, for Fred was an ex-guide who had cut his professional teeth on the West Coast, not an easy fishery, and known for small numbers of large fish and crowds of anglers trying to catch them. Against such odds and inconveniences, Fred refined his skills and local knowledge to such a high degree he said he could guarantee a double-figure fish if a client was with him for more than just a couple of days.

No, he said, he genuinely liked to catch big fish for no reason other than they presented a greater challenge, especially if you weren't just lucky but consistent in catching them. But I had to be sure he really meant it, so I told him about one 'double' I got in the Karamea catchment in Kahurangi National Park. I told him how it was a long and fishless walk until I spotted the leviathan, how I caught and released him, and how the whole thing happened so quickly and unexpectedly, only moments later I began to doubt if it had happened at all. To make sure I was not hallucinating, alone in the bush, I sniffed the net, and yes, it did smell of fish, but it never occurred to me to even take pictures of that trout, not wanting the entire sensory experience to be tainted by the need of acquiring a proof. It was between me and the fish, I said, and Fred assured me he knew exactly what I was talking about.

That evening, after dinner, we sat on the riverbank smoking fat Nicaraguan cigars, a duty-free luxury which Fred had reserved for après-fish celebrations. His seemed a touch undeserved, since when we arrived at the pool the big fish was not there. But Fred did not mind that, either. There would be others, plenty of others. Catching them was not a question of luck but of skill and preparation.

From that moment on I knew that, as our mutual friend had foreseen in his greater wisdom, I would indeed get on well with Fred, especially if we hunted big fish together. I began to ply him with questions, studying his approach to the quest. It was apparent there was much to be learned and understood here.

First it was his gear. Little wonder he did not like to catch smaller fish, because a trout of 3 or 4 lbs would not put much of a bend in his seven-weight rod — a piece of equipment most anglers would use on the Tongariro, but certainly not on a creek or a small river. His leader was twice the length of his big-fish rod, and the heavier of the nymphs was the equivalent of an epoxy bomb. The other, the one that did the fishing, and the catching, was an imitation of a mayfly nymph, small and slim, and convincingly realistic.

As you can imagine, such a rig posed some interesting casting challenges, and when Fred readied his line he would roll-cast it with a powerful log-splitting chop, and there would be a distinct and almost unnaturally long pause, then the sound of a dive-bombing magpie as the big nymph caught up with the rest of the line. The bomb needed a lot of line to carry it and to load the rod, and once the whole show was in the air and Fred's eyes on the fish, he would cast a long way ahead and even further beyond his target.

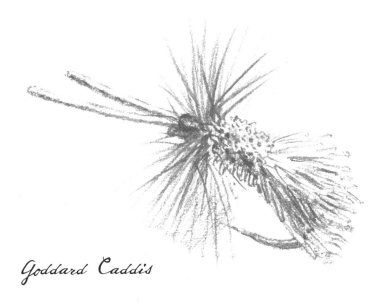

Goddard Caddis

If he left it as it landed, the cast would surely line the fish by metres but as the line settled and began to drift down he would pull it back, adjusting the length just so, throwing the slack part of the line as a mend, up or down stream, as the current dictated.

By the time the whole caboodle reached the fish's window of perception it was drifting perfectly, with just the precise length of line and no visible drag, and at a depth unattainable with a regular rig.

'Big fish are almost always down deep,' Fred said, adding weight to the statement by mentioning that it was so with most of the forty or fifty trophies he had caught so far. 'You also very rarely see them, so if you're after big fish sight-fishing is not the most productive style.'

It was far better to find the most likely deep water and fish it blind, or come back at night and pull a deer-hair mouse across it. His recipe for stripping the line with a mouse pattern at the end — slow-slow-FAST, short-short-LONG — sounded like something out of the *Kama Sutra.*

I was eager to see this style of fishing in action, and we agreed to meet a few days later in Manapouri. We pondered the satellite weather maps and picked the perfect day for our sortie. At first, it was going to be the upper Oreti River, nowadays everyone's big fish Mecca, but lately Fred had been biased towards sea-run trout, and so he picked the mouth of the Waiau instead.

If you think you have river trout figured out, then going after sea-run fish throws a few more variables into the equation.

First, there are tides to reckon with, along with cloud cover
and moon phases. Then there is the presence or lack of smelt
and whitebait which are the main attractors for the silver trout.
I guess most anglers would be happy just to go in and chance
their luck, but for Fred the variables were like pieces of a puzzle
which, when properly put together, would make up a picture — a
formula — for catching big sea-runs consistently.

'Anyone can get lucky once or twice,' he said. 'I want to
understand the sea-runs, figure them out, so that catching them is
not so much the matter of luck but skills and timing.'

My sentiments exactly, though that day on the Waiau they were
to be put to a severe test.

It started off well enough. 'This is the best river in the world,'
a talkative local in camo gumboots told us on arrival. 'It has trout
and sea-runs, whitebait and salmon, even kahawai. What else
would you want?'

Well, how about getting any of these, except the whitebait, to
take a fly?

The place was as spectacular as it was harsh. The rest of
the country basked in sunshine and stillness, the upper Oreti
including, but this south coast was hemmed in by clouds, grey
and heavy. The ocean surf pounded the gravel beach, and a stiff
wind stirred dust devils of coarse sand until they chased each other
across the dunes. Old whitebaiting caravans and shacks littered
the riverbank, their colours faded or stripped by the relentless
salt-blasting winds. There was an edge-of-the-world feeling to
this coast, similar to what you might feel in Patagonia, and this, in
Fred's mind, made for promising fishing.

We crossed an estuary channel and I let the dog loose, and in no
time she barked herself hoarse at the seagulls, which taunted her,
croaking and squawking at her, hovering in the stiff breeze just out
of range of her jumps. There was good structure to the river — a
wide, sweeping gravel bend with a pronounced and stable drop-
off, a tidal shelf that would be good for spotting, a riffle, pool and
a braid with defined feed lines.

We tied on smelt imitations and began to fish, and I realised
immediately I'd come under-gunned for the conditions. The wind
howled upstream and across us, and turned casting into a punch-
bag workout. Fred had turned around and was casting towards the
bank, then letting his backcast drop on the water, and fishing that.
It was a practical solution, but even so my six-weight rod was too
light to get the line out far enough and in the desired direction.
I heard Fred give a shout, and as I looked up I saw that his rod was

bent. But the fish was small and he released it quickly as if it was a piece of weed stuck on his fly. Moments later he had another one, but it was the same: 9½ lb short of a 10-pounder.

We persevered for most of the day, through both the ebbing and the incoming tide, changing places, lines and flies, trying to make sense of the sea-runs. We didn't, or at least I didn't. I caught one fish that was so small I wasn't sure if it was trying to eat my Silicon Smelt or got hooked while mating with it. The wind never stopped and the big sea-runs never came. I found such fishing intolerably boring — casting at the ocean, hoping to get lucky, a lottery which only a few people bothered to play. In his book *The Longest Silence*, Tom McGuane said he thought this kind of fishing 'required a big arm and a room-temperature IQ', and though I thought it a bit harsh when I read it, I was ready to agree with him now.

I thought of the sunshine on the Oreti and all the other rivers but this one, and I suddenly yearned to see trout through the moving mirror of the water, see them weaving and dancing, suspended in the current the way those seagulls rode the onshore wind. And I prayed: dear God, give me a sunny spring creek any day and I won't care about the size of the fish. Anything but casting at the bleak ocean and into this wind.

At six in the evening I finally accepted defeat. I called in the dog and we made our way back to the truck. Fred stayed on and continued fishing, only making a brief appearance at the camper to suck up one of his freeze-dried meals (he would not waste fishing time on cooking). Then he went back out, not wanting to miss another minute. I fed the dog, then cooked spaghetti with Japanese udon noodles and ate them with red wine, sitting outside in the lee of the camper. I smoked another Nicaraguan cigar and watched the night fall, the sun finally and briefly finding its way through a finger-wide gap between the slab of clouds and the horizon. Fred's cigar would remain untouched again, which was bound to be good for his health. I admired his self-imposed rule of only smoking after a fish of 8 lbs or more, but placed no such limitations on myself. God only knew there were enough rules in the world without me adding another one. Besides, I enjoyed my cigar in the politically correct way: I smoked but did not inhale. What harm could come of that?

Fred came back well after dark.

'Nothing,' he said. 'Didn't quite get it right today. We'll know better next time. Sure to nail a few of the big bad boys here. It's perfect water for that.'

I was sure it was, and I was sure he would nail them. I was just as sure that I wouldn't be there to see it, because I'd be fishing a spring creek somewhere sunny and calm. But I'd love to hear his stories.

If I told you where we fished for three days in mid-December your life would be in danger, because sometimes it can be perilous to know such secrets. In danger, too, would be my own masculinity, for, sure as Sage, my compadres-in-rod would come after me also. So let us just say, after Papa Hemingway, that the river was as big and as wide as a good river should be, and that the ratio of trout to water was favourable, if not to the trout then surely to the angler.

But let us also add, leaving Papa to his vices and devices (since we have long ago moved from impaling grasshoppers on hooks and calling it fly-fishing), that this lower South Island river had enough side-creeks and spring-fed backwaters to provide textbook sight-fishing. This was to be its saving grace during our visit, as the river itself was far from being at its best, running the colour of milk put into a Bombay Sapphire bottle, and so high even some of the side-creeks were marginal to cross in a Landcruiser with the snorkel higher than your head.

There were four of us in that truck. David Lloyd, my regular riverside buddy, was back again from Asia for his fix of fly-fishing, and this time he had brought a friend named Mike Brady, an initiate to this game of trout. Then there was yours truly and Craig Smith, a champion bloke and a competent outdoors all-rounder who once gained notoriety when he wrecked his sea kayak off the coast of Banks Peninsula and saved his life with an epic swim that was front-page news across the district. Craig guides this river regularly if infrequently, and it was his call whether we should attempt the crossings or not.

He tested some of the creeks by wading them all the way across, looking for holes, soft spots and other hazards.

'If I can wade it I can drive it,' he said, and this struck me as a good rule to remember. I had only recently backed off from several such crossings, not so much mistrusting my own Landcruiser but my judgement. Craig's own river sense was finely tuned and tested in battles. After a particularly gnarly crossing, in a place where several years ago a Land Rover was swept away and its driver drowned, he told us how, getting across the Cascade River south of Haast, his truck side-drifted in the current for some ten metres before it clawed its way up and out. Inside the car, both Craig

From this moment on, the fly and the fish were on a collision course and, more than once, the trout was lifting through the column of water — a metre or more — with its mouth already open, an indelible memory.

and his passenger were wearing life jackets, a lesson from another incident in the Cascade when, during a similar crossing, the Nissan 4WD of the local farmer became a river-bottom attraction and, no doubt, a home to eels and trout.

After a few hours of low-range grind we got to our base in an old musterers' hut. Mike and David had each caught 5-lb browns from one of the creeks we fished before we crossed it. Craig and I had landed fish, too, and they had all seemed eager and easy, and we thought it augured well for the trip. If we had only known just how well.

Though the level of our experience varied greatly — it was Mike's first ever fishing trip, while Craig had fished this river for more than a decade, and he had flown into it, and driven and mountain biked and walked its entire length, with David and me falling somewhere in-between, none of us was prepared for the spectacle, the sheer visual impact of fishing to trout which had obviously not seen an angler for a considerable length of time.

You'd think that on a small creek or backwater four would be a crowd, but this time it was not so. Perhaps the rains and spates which had plagued us from the beginning of the season had pushed the fish out of the main flow and into the side-creeks, for we found trout in most pools, either actively nymphing in current bottlenecks and on lips demarcating sudden changes in depth, or lying just under the surface feed line, eyeing all objects passing overhead, some of which were our Wulffs, beetle and cicada imitations.

Each time we spotted a fish there would be the usual overly polite banter as to whose turn it was, and when this was decided the rest of us settled back to watch, as if from ringside seats.

The audience would fall silent, and if the cast was good there were distinct acts to the drama that followed. The fly, usually one of the aforementioned terrestrials, would land with a plop, and as it began to drift downstream we often caught ourselves holding our breaths. There would be a decisive moment when the fish saw the fly, when it recognised it as an article of desire and decided to have it. You could see it in its body language, in the change from the languid and relaxed swaying in the current to a snap of senses and a sudden tension — the excitement and anticipation of a predator zeroing in on its quarry.

From this moment on, the fly and the fish were on a collision course and, more than once, the trout was lifting through the column of water — a metre or more — with its mouth already open, an indelible memory. As the fish took the fly, there was often an audible smack of its jaws, followed instantly by a chorus of gasps as we spectators finally remembered to breathe. The fights and landings seemed a routine necessity, a wind-down from the climax of the take itself. Only once, a fish Craig hooked in a bush-edge pool tried to wrap him around an underwater boulder, but he followed it valiantly through the deepest water, undoing a knot in the making, eventually netting the fish and giving himself a tidemark that reached well above his hips.

It was almost the end of the day, and one of its last pools, when we came across *my* fish, one that I shall not forget for as long as I can cast a fly. We were walking a high clay bank, a miniature cliff top almost, when all of us saw it simultaneously: a bulky brown shape barely under the surface, where the steep bank and the water met.

There wasn't much spotting involved — the fish stood out like a half-surfaced submarine in an empty seascape — but it was well out of the feed line and did not appear to show any interest in passing food.

'Maybe he needs waking up with a big dry,' David suggested, and we all agreed it was a fine idea. By this time I had become something of the team's sniper, and so I was voted to cast to this fish, even though it wasn't exactly my turn. It would have been undemocratic to argue, and so, on the edge of the high bank, I got down to my knees, pulled enough line off the reel and let the current straighten it downstream.

I am an impassioned unbeliever in false casting, especially when the water is so clear it can make you feel an onset of vertigo when you look into it. I have seen enough touchy fish spook even before the fly landed on the water and they had a chance to see it. What I like to do is to measure out my line, putting one cast well behind

> *As if in suspended animation, the trout pivoted and shot towards the floating Wulff, downstream and across the entire creek, and nabbed the fly with a take as decisive as a punch.*

and to the side of the fish to judge the distances and angles so that the cast that really matters — the first one the trout will see — is as accurate as it can be. This time, too, such an approach seemed a sensible strategy.

And then it happened. My fly landed well downstream of the fish and near the other bank of the creek, more than five metres away, and I was about to pick it up and recast to where I wanted it to go when the fish became visibly agitated. Not spooked — this much we already knew from watching the body language of other fish that day.

As if in suspended animation, the trout pivoted and shot towards the floating Wulff, downstream and across the entire creek, and nabbed the fly with a take as decisive as a punch. The suspense was such that if you'd played the theme music from *Jaws*, with its accelerating heartbeat rhythm, the whole scene could not have been more dramatic. I had enough sense — just — to wait until the fish turned before I lifted the rod and jumped to my feet. The fish exploded out of the water in total surprise at our ruse. I heard yahoos and expletives of jubilation, and I'm sure some of them were mine.

There was nowhere to land the fish for a good 200 metres, and I walked it downstream, holding the rod high, until we could get down the bank, where Mike helped me to net it.

The handshakes and shoulder slaps were hard and earnest, for we knew these were the days of days, and we were drinking them up, and had each other to magnify the experience. On the way back to the hut David remarked: 'It don' matter who catches the fish. All the fish today were mine 'cause I was there, and I saw them take, and it was nothing like I've ever seen.'

Only Mike seemed a bit confused by this fuss. He was clearly happy, but not quite as elated as the rest of us.

'He doesn't know how good this is,' David teased. 'How many people do you know who don't remember how many five-pounders they caught on their first ever day's fly-fishing?'

Mike made a face of surprise.

'You mean it's not like this all the time?'

We laughed at such innocence. He was certainly in for a crash landing when we got back to the real world and normal fishing, but what an introduction to the joys of trout!

At night we ate venison backsteaks, acquired during Craig's most recent foray into the bush, garnished with sautéed asparagus tossed on top of the meat like dishevelled pickup sticks. We had red wine and Isle of Skye peat water, and as we sat around the open fire, long silences began to creep into the conversation as each of us, in the privacy of his own mind, was already replaying the memory clips from the past two days, each clip a trophy and a keeper.

Then something distracted us. It was a faded picture hanging above the fireplace. It showed an old man holding a trophy trout, long and fat like a distended football, and the engraved plaque explained that the man, one John F. Aitken, now deceased, fished and loved this river for fifty years.

Above the picture, crossed like real-life coat-of-arms weapons, were two fishing rods, presumably his, and stuck into the guide eye of one of them was a stub of a cigar, thick as a thumb, burnt out and extinguished like the man's life itself. A golden band proclaiming it was a Macanudo, a Dominican brand, ringed it like a signet. We assumed the cigar was his, too — either the last one he smoked, or his favourite brand, it did not matter.

What mattered was the thought of what it would be like to fish a river like this for fifty years, to get to know its moods and secrets the way Roderick Haig-Brown got to know his Campbell; this river which, after only two days of fishing it, we already considered the best we'd ever known.

'Imagine what this river must be like when it's clear and in condition,' I ventured, and David replied, 'It'd be a shame not to come back and find out.'

Same time next year? It was settled.

January

HAVE YOU EVER BEEN ON A FISHING TRIP, long planned and much anticipated, where nothing seems to go right for you? You arse up just stepping out of the helicopter and give yourself a good one on the shin, a bruise that over the following days blossoms plump and purple like a Baccara rose. And that's just the beginning.

You promptly trump this with another act, stepping on the loose end of a vine with one foot, with the other tripping over the noose you've thus created. You want to break the fall with your hands, but they are full of camping gear and heavy supermarket bags, and your backpack, well, it's just big and inert enough to prevent a recovery.

Your companions help you up and give you puzzled looks. They are probably thinking: 'What's up with him? We all like a good drink but this is ridiculous. It's not even lunchtime yet.' And you, too, wonder: what the hell is going on? Is this me or some nasty taniwha whose home ground I have just entered and who clearly does not want me here?

Soon enough you're convinced it's probably both, because things get worse from there. On the river, you tangle up repeatedly, spook every trout you see, hook yourself with your own fly, and naturally it is one of only a handful in the fly box that have not been de-barbed.

To further compound the aggravation, your companions are having the time of their lives. That first night in the headwaters of the Rangitikei, one of the best and most remote of the North Island backcountry rivers, after we set up a camp of three tents and a large 'living room' tarp in the forest clearing, Michel Dedual trotted off for an evening hunt and only ten minutes up the creek bagged a decent-sized sika deer. He brought it down, dressed and hung it inside a large mesh meat safe, then, going down to the creek to wash his hands, he spotted a fish rising in the camp pool. He ran up to get his rod, ran back, and hooked the 6-lb trout with his first cast. In the pool below, I was with Marc, watching him hook and fight an equally magnificent rainbow. When night fell all I had to show for the day was a limp, a grazed elbow, and an increasingly foul mood.

But then we were all three back in the camp, and the fire, wine and good food worked their purifying wizardry. I stared into the flames, sipping another glass of red, and thought: 'Hey, anyone can have a false start, a bad day, and mine was just about over.' Earlier, I had poured some wine on the dry ground and the beech leaves that cushioned it, a kind of peace offering to the taniwha, if there was one. You never know, better safe than sorry. I certainly did not want to fight it for another day, or fight my ten-thumbs, two-left-feet self.

The upper Rangitikei, clear as spring water, snakes a contorted passage through the volcanic hills of the Kaimanawa Forest Park, east of the Tongariro River. The fishing here is hard and honest at the best of times, without added challenges or handicaps. You don't come here to 'clean up pools'. Every fish is a hard win, a major victory, and that's providing you are at your best, assertive and sharp. Tomorrow, I promised myself, was a fresh start, a *tabula rasa* I would fill with perfect first casts and beautiful fighting fish. No pratfalls and blunders. No goof-ups. No excuses. I fell asleep with visions of rainbows racing each other to take those beautiful CDC dries Marc was tying.

I have to tell you about Marc. This, after all, was his trip, his story. He had travelled halfway around the world for these five days on the Rangitikei, and Michel especially did all in his considerable power to make them a memorable outing, at least as far as

> *Though we had brought with us enough flies to start a riverside tackle shop, in the end these two patterns were the only ones we would use. The Rangitikei fish either took them within the first couple of casts, or took nothing at all.*

organising went. Once on the river Marc needed no help at all. As Pasteur said, 'Good fortune favours the prepared mind', and Marc Petitjean was more prepared than most. 'If you define the problem, the solution is often obvious,' he told me that first night, apropos of nothing. 'People often get pissed off with themselves, and they don't know why. They never take time to precisely identify what bugs them. If they did, the remedy would be self-evident.'

These were wise words, but they were lost on me at the time.

Next morning, while doing the dishes on the riverbank, I scooped a large mayfly nymph — probably a *Nesameletus* — out of the river and into my stainless steel mug. It was hard not to. The aquatic insect life in the Rangitikei is so prolific that every time you dip a pot, plate or even cupped hands in the water you're likely to capture one or more of the little beasts. No wonder the trout grow so large here.

I took the mug with the critter swimming in circles along the bottom back to the camp. Marc examined it closely, then set up his tying vice and whipped up a dozen or so imitations in three sizes, with tungsten heads and all-CDC bodies. Then he tied a handful of CDC dries, his generic mayfly pattern with an added white parachute post for high visibility. These would serve us as indicators, with the post made from the tail hair of the sika deer that was hanging from a nearby tree. Though we had brought with us enough flies to start a riverside tackle shop, in the end these two patterns were the only ones we would use. The Rangitikei fish either took them within the first couple of casts, or took nothing at all.

After Marc had his nymph pattern figured out, Michel Dedual, a Turangi fisheries scientist and the nemesis of red and sika deer, wild pigs and Taupo trout, took the mug back to the river, a walk of some 20 metres or so, and upended it, releasing the critter back into its home water, muttering something about *la pauvre bête*. It was a small gesture, but a telling one. I knew that, taniwhas or my own demons notwithstanding, I was in fine company.

We were fishing in French. This was only natural, since both Marc and Michel come from the French-speaking Swiss canton of Fribourg, and I once lived not far from there and have always been something of a closet Francophile — even when, after the *Rainbow Warrior* and Chirac's follies at Mururoa, the simple act of buying ink cartridges for a French-made fountain pen in New Zealand was considered an act of national treason.

It is an obscure and oft-overlooked historical fact — a classic case of the butterfly effect — that if, at the decisive moment of the European colonisation of the Pacific, a certain Monsieur Langlois had driven his whaling ship *Cachalot* with just a little bit more haste, the way the French usually drive, the South Island could well have been not part of the Commonwealth but the Nouvelle-France of the South. Imagine that. We could have had topless beaches and chocolate from the Côte d'Or, *bœuf braisé* and *coq au vin* instead of pies and KFC, *champignons* instead of mushrooms, vineyards as thick as native forests and scholarships at La Sorbonne. The two islands would be like England and France, with the Cook Strait for the Channel. How different things could have been . . . how *drôle*! At times, I still feel a certain *nostalgie* for such scenario.

I have also always had a fondness for French fishermen and women because most of those I've met have in small or profound ways influenced my own way of fly-fishing. I've yet to meet a French angler who was a hack, whose casting was less than masterly, whose fly box wasn't a treasure trove of ideas and surprises. Whatever they do, the French usually do it with passion and abandon, and these they match with an overkill of skill and the best and most innovative gear money can buy. You'd be hard pushed to find a better example of all that than Marc Petitjean.

French born but living and working in Switzerland, Petitjean is the man responsible for the modern-day renaissance of CDC flies, both dries and nymphs, and especially the CDC-only flies which are one of his own contributions to our art and pursuit. When he is tying, his hands are a blur, a testimony to some 25,000 flies he has produced each year for the past decade, using up over a quarter tonne of *Croupion de Canard* (bastardised into *Cul de Canard*, *cul* being a slang word for the backside, where the duck's waterproofing gland is located). Think about it: a quarter tonne of CDC is a quack-load of ducks.

A remote Fiordland stream and one of the treasures it holds.

Ian Cole reflects on the selection of his favourite still-water flies: damsel nymph, bloodworm, Black & Peacock and a water boatman.

David Lloyd poised for a take on
La Fontaine (top), Stu Tripney's
'rubber legs' nymph (middle),
and the prize when it all comes
together (bottom).

A good guide like Craig Smith is always there for you: heading off a runaway fish (top), catching you when you fall (middle), and taking the best care of the quarry (bottom).

Quintessential New Zealand backcountry: freedom to roam, solitude and always the chance of a big fish. Mops taking a spell in the shade from the mid–summer heat.

South of Haast the trout country is swampy and
challenging to get around (top right) often calling
for ingenious transport arrangements (top left).
The rewards can be explosive, though with the odds
stacked heavily in the trout's favour, good teamwork
is often essential.

Finally, a hook–up with a Coloburiscus dry fly. Lower Arnold River, South Island's West Coast.

Johnny Groome on his beloved Arnold, one of the best trout waters in the world most anglers have never heard about.

Apart from earning himself the title 'the pope of CDC', Marc has brought a Swiss-army-knife style of technology and engineering to the world and the fly-tying bench of anglers. His vice, vest and fly-tying accessories and tools, after you've seen them for the first time, instantly fall into a must-have category, if you're lucky enough to obtain them. His bobbin holders, for example, as easy to thread as striking a match, are in such demand he cannot produce enough of them. And now, from first-hand experience, I can tell you he is as good an angler as he is an engineer and inventor. Watching him fish, laying out long and accurate casts and adjusting them just so with measured mends, is as pleasurable as doing it yourself. In my sorry asinine state on the Rangitikei, it was actually better than doing it myself.

In the morning we started up the river, zigzagging against its meanders, linking up shoulder to shoulder for the crossings, stalking the tails and eyes of every pool. The middle parts of pools, sandy, deep and slow-moving, were impossible. The fish, like submarines, were either parked right at the bottom or finned leisurely in circles, nymphing among the dust devils of debris, completely out of reach. With good sunlight, against the background of mossy cliffs and forest, the fish were easy to see, but catching one — well, for the first few hours at least it seemed beyond the ability of any of us.

Though the water was not yet heavily fished this season — only a few parties had visited thus far — the trout were exceptionally wary, probably due more to the water clarity than angling pressure. Browns you could not touch. Even lifting a rod to initiate a cast was enough to send them off at speed. Rainbows were more forgiving, but only slightly. One in three or four fish offered what I'd consider a fair chance of being caught, and these odds did not take into account human error or gaucherie.

With three of us on the river, I had only two opportunities that day. On the first I hung up a cast, and by the time I untangled my line the fish was gone. On the second, an unexpected gust of downstream wind doubled back my 16-foot leader and dumped it on top of the fish. It was like throwing a rock at it: one moment it was there, the next it was gone, dematerialised. Was this mongrel of a taniwha still following me? I gritted my teeth and took solace in watching the faultless travails of my companions. Despite heavy odds to the contrary, Marc eked out two beautiful fish, and Michel had another one. This, the latter assured us, was really good going in the Rangitikei. And all this happened even before the godsend of the evening rise.

Even if the fishing is hard, the Rangitikei offers a saving grace in the form of an evening mayfly hatch. Fish that are so difficult during the day are suddenly bolder and more visible, and just careless enough to be humbugged. Thus a skunk here is not really a skunk until the night falls fully. Even if you have not touched a thing all day, you can relax in the confidence that the half hour of twilight during the evening rise should produce opportunities which can be converted into fish with even a modicum of skill. Unless, of course, you have your demons for company, or make a cock-up of a stratagem, like I did that second night.

On the classic South Island dry-fly rivers I fish regularly, you can assume that, if there's going to be an evening rise, it'll happen in the slower, smoother bottom third of the pool. I am not quite sure why it is so, whether this is where the mayflies are more likely to hatch, or perhaps where the fish can see them better. But you can bank on it, especially if, along the deeper side of the river, there are defining features like trailing willow branches or bushes which create a funnel-like effect in the feed line. This is the spot the best fish would dominate, a place of primary focus for an observant angler.

So that night, as we divided a long cliff pool into thirds so each of us had enough room to fish, I took the bottom section and, all gear ready and double-checked, set out to wait.

And wouldn't you know it, the Rangitikei trout do not rise in the tail of the pool. They rise at the top end, just below the white water of the riffle. In the dimming twilight some fifty metres above me I heard a heavy splash, then Michel's laughter echoed down off the cliff bank.

'Hah! She is a beauty, this one!'

It wasn't long before Marc had a fish on, too, then Michel again. In the space of an intense few minutes they landed half a dozen fine rainbows, while absolutely nothing was happening at my end.

It was almost dark when, finally — *Mon Dieu!* Was this really possible? — a fish rose some ten metres in front of me. I'd been ready for the past half hour, line coiled at my feet, fly kept dry in my left hand, and so instantly I had the dainty CDC with its white punk hairdo in the trout's window of vision. Another rise. I held off for just a moment then gingerly lifted the rod. There was a violent tug back against my pull, then, where the rise had been, a hefty fish leaped, flashing silver against the gloom of the forested cliffs. It bounced off the surface and jumped higher still, then buried deep into the inky water, tearing off all the loose line I had at my feet and a goodly length from the reel as well.

Now I had it on the reel, in control. My throat went lumpy and dry. Man, finally. I had a fish on. I was back. Back from the lala-land of botchery and blunder. And not a moment too soon. This place was far too special, too once-in-a-lifetime kind of water to fish it like a twonk.

I reeled in some line, and the fish pulled it back, and I gained it again. The reel sang, these were the sweetest moments. And then, would you believe it, the fish broke me off. Just like that. Twang! What was touted as 'the world's strongest fluorocarbon' snapped like the tying thread pulled too tight. I wanted to sit down on the bank and howl.

The campfire evening, like the one before, was a respite from my growing despair. Marc entertained us with his stories of fishing around the world, of his cavalier days as a horse-riding stuntman (the French have a beautiful word for that: *le cascadeur*, from *cascade*, to fall tumbling; in a word, someone who is paid to fall), and, of course, the history of the *cul de canard* and his own journey of discovery into its properties.

It appears that CDC flies have always been something of a French-Swiss speciality. Fribourg is not far from Vallorbe, a town where the *Moustique du Jura* (the Jura Mosquito, a.k.a. the Vallorbe fly) first 'hatched' in the vice of one Maximilien Joset sometime in the 1920s. Or possibly another local, Charles Bickel, was the first to tie them. Or perhaps the two men invented them simultaneously but independently of each other, no one can tell for sure. But undoubtedly it was in the low-lying limestone mountains of the Jura, and their rivers known for small but difficult brown trout, where it all began.

From there the CDC story, as pursued by Marc Petitjean, moved to Marjan Fratnik, a fisherman of the Slovenian rivers (notably the Soca) and their marbled trout, who came up with the Fratnik Fly, or the F-FLY. Over the years, others added their small refinements until Marc himself had a revelation.

So far, CDC was added to float flies made with more traditional materials. But Marc thought, why not make flies exclusively with CDC? After all, it was a perfect material: light, dense, naturally buoyant and lifelike, aerodynamic to the point that it folded up streamlined during the cast, then sprang open again as the line slowed down, parachuting the fly so it landed in a most natural way. That thought was the beginning of the modern CDC revolution, and also of Petitjean Fishing Equipment, a top-end boutique business which has been keeping Marc occupied since 1986.

'It was a liberating idea,' he told us. 'Suddenly, you didn't need a hackle to float a fly. The CDC body would do it. And then I thought, why not make CDC nymphs as well; they look and behave so much more lifelike than those made from other materials. On it went from there: Magic Tool and split threads, CDC oil, flies for salmon, bonefish, bass and tarpon. You've seen how well the flies work. People convert to them the moment they see them in action.'

True enough, the night before our departure for the Rangitikei we had helped to set up one of three fly-tying demonstrations Marc was giving in New Zealand, this one at the National Trout Centre south of Turangi. The Taupo fishing folk have their ways and preferences, and small dry fly is not among these, so the first part of Marc's instructive show, supplemented with a large-screen video close-up of his hands at work, was received politely but without much enthusiasm. Only when he started tying streamers, especially the white-marabou smelt pattern featuring his Magic Head at the front of the hook, that someone asked: 'What's the little umbrella for?'

'You'll see soon enough,' Marc said, and indeed, the audience was in for a surprise. The Magic Head is a tiny silicon funnel the size of your pinkie nail which, when cut to shape and balanced with the rest of the streamer, imparts a remarkably lifelike side-to-side movement to the fly as it is stripped through the water. It works particularly well with the marabou, which fluffs up every time the fly stops.

Later that night, there were gasps of awe and disbelief in the crowd lining the bank of the centre's trout pond as Marc pulled his smelt fly through the water, illuminated by a single video light on a high stand. One gentleman, whose visiting card proclaimed him a 'trout-fishing enthusiast' almost had to be restrained to prevent him from jumping into the pool after the fly.

'This is remarkable,' he kept repeating. 'In all my years of fishing I've never seen an artificial fly look so realistic. What'd you say this little umbrella was called? Can I buy some straight away?'

Just like that, all the Magic Heads were sold out, and a back-order list started to fill up. As Marc said, you had to see it to believe it, but once you saw it you didn't want to use anything else.

Next morning we packed for an overnight bivvy and headed back up the river, bypassing the section we had already fished. Upstream, the trout were as unapproachable as ever, feeding

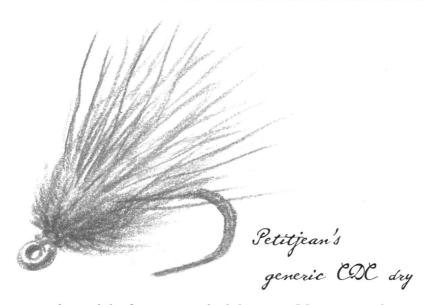

Petitjean's generic CDC dry

voraciously until the first cast touched the water. We saw a couple
of trophy browns moving in formation, but they swam past us in
what can only be described as contempt, right past Marc's perfectly
presented flies, past our feeble efforts to camouflage ourselves
against the bankside forest.

I plodded half-heartedly behind the others, deriving what
pleasure I could from watching them fish. They were getting
better, if that were possible, becoming attuned to the river, and
their odds on a fish were now 50/50, often better. I had hooked
a nice fish early in the morning — first cast, positive take, no
problems. But then, you see, the little steel Mikro ring which
connects the leader to the fluorocarbon tippet, well, it . . . Yeah, I
wouldn't believe that either.

Still, there was the sure-bet evening rise, the pools above us
untouched by an angler for days, if not weeks. This time, fortune
favouring the prepared, etc, I decided I'd have a whole pool to
myself. If we shared one I was sure to draw the short straw again.
I examined the pool near where we were to camp — long, deep,
well-structured, sure to be a home to several fish, judging by the
numbers we were seeing below — and claimed it for myself.

Michel approved of my choice. 'You're right, this is a very good
pool,' he said. 'Every evening I've spent here we've caught some
really good fish in it. Break your rod, huh.' Having wished me luck
in that peculiarly superstitious European way, he and Marc went a
couple of pools upstream, and I was left alone.

From plentiful and bone-dry driftwood I built a small fire
away from the river, and much later, after it got completely dark,

I watched the lights of my friends' two head torches groping their way back down and across the river, wobbling out of sync during each crossing, navigating their way towards my fire.

'How did it go?' I asked when they arrived.

'*Fabuleux!*' Marc exulted. 'We had a double.'

'A ten-pounder?'

'No, a double hook-up,' he corrected. 'We got others, too, four or five altogether. And you?'

Well, what could I say? Not a single fish had risen in Michel's never-fail pool. It was as if the trout, normally plentiful here, took offence when I showed up.

The most troubling thing of all was that, by now, I was not even surprised. If we had had a radio, I was ready to call in a chopper and end this agony. It would have been an expensive if merciful and deserved *coup de grâce*. But, until our pre-arranged pick-up date, we were incommunicado, and as it turned out, just as well.

The night was rough. It started to rain, first softly, then harder. The tarp was small and sagged on both sides, despite our best efforts to make it taut. The wind flapped it all night and, weighted with rain, the fabric stuck to the sleeping bags of those bedding on each side. Inexplicably, I had the dry and protected middle bunk. A token consolation in my misery.

It was cosy enough under the small tarp with the three of us, but as the thrumming of rain intensified, two very wet dogs — my Airedale and Michel's wire-hair Yoga — crawled under the tarp, too. They found the only vacant spaces and expanded into them the way sealant fills the gaps between floorboards. Neither pleas nor threats, nor even an execution of the latter would make them leave. They dug in their eight feet in protest, their bodies suddenly impossibly heavy to shift. This was not what you'd call passive resistance or sudden deafness to all commands but, well, a dogged determination that, no matter what, they were not going back outside and into the rain. It was a position hard to argue with, when you are groggy with sleep.

Despite everything, I slept well. Better than for many nights past, totally at peace with myself. The previous evening by the fire, while the others feared their rods may be breaking from the strain of fighting fish, I had had a little tête-à-tête with my demon.

All things considered, I started off reasonably enough.

'Listen, you son of a bitch,' I said, 'enough is enough. I can take a day of this, two days max, but not the whole fricken trip. I have travelled a long way for this. Not as far as Petitjean, but Wanaka is not exactly around the corner, you know. This country is not large, but by god isn't it long? Like three full days' drive long. So why don't you just lay off and let a guy catch himself a fish or two. Stop being such a sadist.'

Word by word, I worked myself into quite a soliloquy. Okay, I admitted, I've been a scatterbrain lately — absent-minded, distracted, never quite there. I had my reasons — hell, just living on this runaway planet is sometimes reason enough — but I'd come here to soothe and heal my rough edges, not to aggravate them further. I went on, unloading my sorrows and grievances, after a time to no one in particular. It was like a psychotherapy session minus the shrink. I believe the North American Indians call this sort of thing a sweat lodge, only they really sweat their stuff, doing it all in a kind of steam sauna, while I only had my fire.

I don't know if this in any way defined my problem, made the solution obvious and self-evident, as Marc avowed, but I woke up feeling fresh and free. Michel whipped up porridge and I made coffee, and we had them standing, already dressed in our waders and rain jackets. The weather was clearing slowly, and overhead spells of brilliant sunshine alternated with squalls and showers.

The overnight rain had discoloured the water just enough that we could still see the fish but they, it seemed, could no longer see the tippets and the ruse of the drifting artificials. Marc and Michel quickly had a fish each, then there was a long barren stretch without much holding water.

Partway through it we hesitated whether to go on. It was nearly midday, and we had a long descent back to the base camp still ahead of us. The visibility was poor at times. Gusts of wind played havoc with casts, often spooking the fish, and the windward side of the valley was darkened by another wave of rain. Both Marc and Michel were happy to head back. Over the past days they had racked up an impressive tally of fish, and me, well, I'd sort of given up ever catching one here. The trip was almost over anyway. The chopper would come to pick us up tomorrow midday.

Still, we lingered, teetering in indecision. Was it really it then? The end?

But then someone said, 'Well, hell, why not? Let's go up another couple more pools,' and this, I now see, really tipped the balance of events. It was a turning point of sorts, clear and obvious, but only with the benefit of hindsight.

We were coming to the first large pool in a while, when from up ahead Michel called: 'Dereque! Here's one for you. He's taking everything that's passing by.'

Great, I thought. How's that for show of confidence in my skills.

But maybe I needed a fish like that, a real dumbo, one that would take a cigarette butt if you floated it past.

I got into position, took a deep steadying breath and cast. There was not the slightest hesitation in the trout's swaying dance. It took my nymph, then another natural, then another still, then, suddenly feeling the tension of my line, erupted out of the water. It jumped again and again, flapping all the way up, like a salmon trying to leap over an obstacle. Wonder of wonders, nothing went wrong. The knots held, the tippet held, the hook did not come out, there were no tangles. I beached him in a little bay of sand near the tail of the pool, a solid Rangitikei rainbow, all chrome and crimson fire, then almost reverently unhooked him and let him slip back into the deep. He was gone in a flash and I was left panting and shaky-handed, still on my knees in the sand.

I stood up and heard Michel laugh. He was hooked to a fish and briskly leading it downstream, with Marc hotfooting in pursuit, taking pictures. Wanting to be alone with this inner glow of the experience for just a few more moments, I picked up my rod and went upstream to where the pool was narrower, the water faster. There I saw it, at the bottom, between two boulders so big they squeezed the current into a sort of doorway. In the middle of it was another fish, a long dark smudge, soft and swaying with exquisite fluidity.

I was strangely calm, absolved from my dog days of bad luck and gaucherie, with a mind that was pure and unafraid of screwing up again. I put a single cast ahead of the two boulders and the fast broken water disguised the plop of the nymph. As if in slow motion, I watched the fish veer slightly to my side and take something, the white tuft of the indicator being sucked under, then I was running downstream, picking my way over the rough boulder field, taking up the slack as I ran. My line wrapped around the reel handle but I caught it just in time, and I had the fish on the reel now, sword-fighting it left and right, counteracting its furious runs.

Then I was kneeling over it in the same sandy bay at the tail of the pool and I felt my companions peering over my shoulder.

'*Très bien fait!*' Marc enthused. '*Fabuleux!*'

'You ever caught a fish that big?' Michel asked, a lopsided grin stretching his moustache.

'Well, sure . . . ' I started, but only now, with adrenalin levels subsiding, I took a good look at my trout. Not that it was particularly long, but it was deep and broad, with the brilliant metallic skin that seemed too small for it.

'How heavy you think he is?' I asked.

'A ten,' Michel said.

'You sure?' I was incredulous.

'Ah, easily.'

All three of us had long ago dispensed with carrying scales, so there was no way of verifying this.

'I think you can trust his judgement,' Marc said later, and I had to agree. In his work as a trout scientist for the Taupo fishery, monitoring several fish traps on the Tongariro catchment, Michel gets to handle and weigh a hell of a lot of trout.

But I shall never know for sure if the fish was a double, and maybe it's better that way. It was certainly the biggest fish of the trip. Until we went up to the next pool.

French is a beautifully musical and expressive language, and it lends itself to many things, especially to swearing. I often think it is worth learning it just so you can use it for this express purpose. The swear words are rarely rude, but they come together in evocative combinations which have an explosive power to convey an outburst of any emotion. As the villain in one of the *Matrix* movies says, swearing in French is like wiping your butt with silk.

Michel, as usual, was at the head of our trio when he called out to us: 'Don't come too close. I've got a good one here.'

There was a wall of thicket between us and him and the river, and he was already in position, stripping line off the reel, preparing to cast. I edged in closer, and through a window in the scrub peered at the fish. It was huge, visibly bigger than mine from only minutes ago. Just seeing it there made me conclude my long-standing debate with 'Fiordland Fred'. He was right, partly. Bigger was not always better, but, on the whole, big was good.

Michel was getting ready to cast when it started.

'*Ah nom de dieu, nom de dieu, quel bordel saloperie,*' I heard him swear, and had to suppress a laugh. He was getting hopelessly tangled up in the matagouri before he had made even a single false cast.

There were sounds of exasperated huffing from where he was, and bushes moved slightly as he retraced his leader through their thorns. The fish continued to feed unperturbed and soon he was ready again.

'Ahhhh!' came his sudden intake of breath. '*Mais purée de merde!*'

A longer pause this time. More untangling.

It was endearing, watching the Monsieur fisheries scientist,

PhD and all, about to cast to the largest fish any of us had seen for a long time, and coming apart a little at the seams, fumbling with his flies and line like a debutant.

Finally, silence. A swish of one good steeple cast, the plop of the nymph, and our world stood still as we watched the indicator approaching the trout. I so wanted him to catch that fish that when the dry fly suddenly vanished an involuntary cry escaped me.

'He's on!'

But he wasn't on. As Michel lifted his rod, the flies and the line came free into the air and he had to kill it all downstream to avoid those dreaded thorn bushes behind him.

The fish continued to feed and Michel made another cast. Perfect. *Comme il faut.*

The indicator dipped and he struck, but again it was nothing, though this time the fish was suddenly no longer there. It vanished like a phantom.

Michel let out a sigh and reeled in his line and we joined him on the bank, sitting down on the rocks, feeling oddly heavy-limbed.

'He is tight-lipped, this one,' Michel said, then he grinned. 'You know, this is my twelfth time up here, and every time this fish has been in this pool, and each time we've tried to catch him, and he always gets the better of us. He's grown bigger over the years, and I hope he gets a bit senile in his old age. That's the only way we'd get a chance to catch him.'

The last morning, while Michel volunteered to take down the camp, I walked with Marc up a tributary which entered the main river not far from our tents. We did not see a fish, but, casting blind into the most likely spot, Marc managed a solid hook-up and landed one more splendid rainbow. At this we took down our rods. The helicopter would be coming soon; it was time to go.

But before we left, we each took a handful of creek water and touched the hands together like goblets, then drank the cold, soft liquid: a toast to the Rangitikei. I spilled some of mine on to the ground as another offering, this time not to appease but to thank. The demons, whether they were local or brought here by me, were as playful as they were generous. Their pranks and antics — and I still bear the scars — really made my trip.

'Yous fellas fishin'?' a Maori guy on the shore of Lake Otamangakau asked. I said we were having a look.

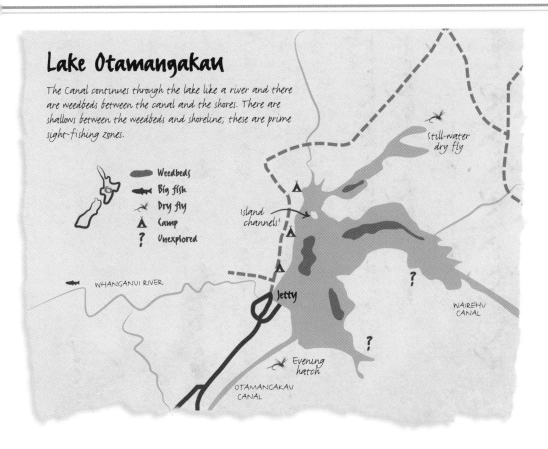

Lake Otamangakau

The Canal continues through the lake like a river and there are weedbeds between the canal and the shores. There are shallows between the weedbeds and shoreline; these are prime sight-fishing zones.

- Weedbeds
- Big fish
- Dry fly
- ⌂ Camp
- ? Unexplored

still-water dry fly

island channels!

WHANGANUI RIVER

Jetty

?

WAIREHU CANAL

?

Evening hatch

OTAMANGAKAU CANAL

'Plenty a fish here, bro. Big bastards, too. But bloody hard to catch, eh?' He was lean and hard, dressed in a bush shirt and hunting shorts, both of which had a lived-in, heavy-use look, and his legs and arms were scratched with bush lawyer and blackberries, the barbed wire of the backcountry. Behind him was a camp that looked like a mobile butcher's workshop. Next to an old-style calico tent, a tarp lean-to and a stainless-steel log burner, game carcasses wrapped in fine white muslin against the blowflies were hung from meat hooks on all available trees. On one of the logs that served as campfire chairs his companion sat pulling an oily swab through the barrel of a large-calibre rifle.

The man's summary of fishing at the lake — big, challenging trout and plenty of them — was precisely what had attracted us here. Sure enough, we saw the first fish — a large shape shadowing against a patch of dark-gold sand — as soon as we reached the waterline. Marc Petitjean was with me, but even his masterly casts and best-money-can-buy flies made no impression on this or any other fish we saw. The trout were wary, not so much spooking but shying from casts and flies, not giving us even one honest opportunity.

Marc made a face of mock dejection. 'This lake is not a place for a casual drive-by fishing,' he said. 'It needs to be studied and understood before anything of consequence happens here.' He couldn't have known it, but this was exactly what I had planned for the next few days. For now, we were just filling a couple of hours before Marc's afternoon flight to Christchurch, where he was to give one last fly-tying demo, then returning home to Fribourg. Before we left for the airport, I went back to the Maori hunters to ask them if there was anywhere nearby I could camp.

'You can camp with us, bro,' one of them said. 'Plenty a room.'

And so it began, my affair with the big O and the whanau that camps along its shores.

I dropped Marc off at the terminal, then went to pick up a boat. With just enough foresight, I had borrowed a three-metre inflatable tender especially for the Otamangakau, because the lake is an old swamp filled by a hydro scheme, and shoreline fishing is limited to a few small and unconnected beaches. The rest of its shores are boggy and full of holes oozing muck and oily blackwater, quickly discouraging any exploration on foot. By the time I returned, backed in the camper so its rear doors gave out on to the lake, pumped up the boat and tied it to a tree it was already dark. Presently, one of the bros materialised, beer in hand, and unceremoniously put another cold one on the bumper of my truck for me.

'Come and have a feed with us,' he said, and when I joined them by their great incinerator fire he picked up an enamel plate from a sheet of corrugated iron that served as a dish-drying rack and heaped it with venison steaks and token stalks of boiled broccoli. Then he took a dinged-up mug, half filled it with Jim Beam and handed them both to me. We ate in contented silence, the lake behind us so still that even the stars reflecting in it did not shimmer. These two, I thought to myself, were my kind of people. My tribe.

In the morning, while I readied for the first exploratory recce of the lake and its trout, the fellas were already off hunting. This, it turned out, they did every day, leaving around 4 a.m., usually bagging something at first light, returning to the camp around 9 a.m., a day's work already accomplished. They rarely came back empty-handed. If it wasn't a red deer or two, it was a wild pig or, once, a five-foot eel which instantly triggered memories of a trip into the Amazon and the anaconda I'd seen there. Later in the day, they often left the camp and went visiting various branches of the whanau: cousins, uncles and nanas, to bestow the gifts of the forest on them. It was summer holidays, the time of reunions, barbecues, hangis and other feasts, and some of the families were hard up. There was nothing like a leg of venison or wild pork chops to put smiles on their faces. My camp fellas seemed to get as big a kick out of that as they did from hunting itself.

The lake, shaped like a deformed three-toed footprint, each toe of different thickness, is a soup of weeds, red, olive and blue damselflies and some 6000 better-than-average brown and rainbow trout. The numbers and sizes of fish are known with a degree of accuracy because to enter the lake all trout have to pass through a fish trap where they are weighed and counted. As I pushed off into the lake that first morning, Michel Dedual's words echoed in my mind: 'Otamangakau is a special place. The fish are big, but they are hard to catch, and harder still to land, so the lake attracts a peculiar breed of anglers, those who have patience and who take pleasure in solving problems and riddles. People either absolutely love it or totally hate it. If you can consistently catch fish in the big O you know you've made your grades as an angler.'

That first day I failed my grades because, true enough, there were problems — many problems — most of them unanticipated. The first and fundamental issue was how to cast effectively from a drifting row boat. This is more complicated than it sounds. The fish I sighted prowling the shallows moved with speed and determination while the boat, too, had its own inertia. The moment I put down the oars to cast, the boat would acquire a mind of its own, pushed and spun around by the wind — it was rare to have a windless day on the O — and it would drift either away from the fish or, worse, directly at and over it. Then, of course, it wasn't enough just to cast a fly to the fish, you had to put it a good few metres ahead, let things settle and wait for the trout to approach, by which time the boat had invariably drifted one way or another, dragging the fly or spooking the fish.

After a morning of frustration and bungled opportunities I rowed back to the camp with a plan in mind. What I needed was a soft, quiet and quickly deployable anchor. This would not stop the boat from spinning — to counteract that you'd need two anchors, fore and aft, and in the time needed to drop both the fish would certainly be gone — but at least it'd stop it from drifting about or away. I found a canvas bag and part-filled it with stones, then attached a length of rope to it which in turn I tied to the transom. After some experimentation I found the most efficient way was to row with the anchor already overboard but above water, holding its coiled rope down with my foot.

> . . . the fish tore out for the open water and I watched the backing vanish from my reel until the spool core was showing, all the while feeling, with even more incredulity, that underneath me the boat, too, was moving, being towed out into the lake by the fish.

When I saw a fish all I had to do was to slowly lift my foot and let the anchor slide down, and this I could do while standing up and getting ready to cast. The timing was critical, as the window of opportunity to present a fly to a cruising fish often lasted only a few seconds. By the first afternoon I was getting better at this juggling of oars, rod and anchor, while calculating the vectors of moving fish, boat and wind, when a dark overcast promptly blew in and covered the lake with white caps. In glary, corrugated water I could not see a thing. I rowed back to the camp. It was clear that sight-fishing the big O required perfect conditions — the right water level, good sunlight, not too much wind — or the already feeble odds would quickly deteriorate into none at all.

Then there was the issue of the tippet. On the second day, hunting the shallows for most of the day and spotting against the background of the swampy shoreline, I managed to hook two fish. This, it turned out, was the easy part of fishing the big O. What followed each time was like an underwater explosion, as if the striking motion of the rod had set off a torpedo to which the boat and I were attached via the fly line.

From the shallows where I hooked them, the fish tore out for the open water and, in disbelief, I watched the backing vanish from my reel until the spool core was showing, all the while feeling, with even more incredulity, that underneath me the boat, too, was moving, being towed out into the lake by the fish. Upon hook-up I had instantly weighed the anchor to have one less thing to tangle up with, but after a few moments of slow biscuiting behind the fish

February

ON THE WAY BACK SOUTH I CAMPED BY
the Motueka River, near its confluence with the
Pearse. The Motueka flows through a stunning
and fertile valley, Arcadian in its feel and
landscape. Steep green hills guide the river, twisting it this
way and that, creating attractive bends, structure and lots of
fishy terrain, while the banks offer kaleidoscopic vistas of
happy rustic lifestyles — orderly orchards and gardens, berry
fields and tree plantations, and here and there unpretentious
whitewashed homes presiding over this valley of plenty.

Yet for all this natural wealth and abundance, and despite
what the trout guidebooks promise here, I have always found
the Motueka a tough place to fish, at times so barren it seemed
completely devoid of life. Over the years, I've put it down
to my own ineptitude and unfamiliarity, the warm water
temperatures and the fact that most pools double as swimming
holes for orchard workers. After several uneventful attempts,
I've given up fishing this river during the day.

But if there is an evening hatch on the Motueka, the fishing can be excellent for an hour or so, and so every time I've passed this way I've timed my travels to arrive well before the sunset, find a good pool, and wait and hope that the mayflies will hatch and the trout will notice. Occasionally, the miracle has happened. With the sunless sky casting the last of its golden sheen on the water, in the feed line against the willows, the fish rise, lining up in their hierarchical order. The bigger fish sip passing mayflies with stately economy, befitting their age and size, making only the tiniest dimples in the surface, while the gung-ho youngsters leap and splash, throwing their entire bodies at the insects, sending sprays of droplets across the river's surface.

Experiencing such a rise is enough to make me forget all previous disappointments and no-shows. I watch and study, compare the rises and choose my fish, always going for the inconspicuous ones, as more often than not they are the most worthwhile opponents.

Casting here requires the utmost precision, for in the prime zone of the feed line the fish are often packed closely one behind another, and you don't want the fly to be snatched by an all-out half-pound youngster before it floats under that overhanging branch where an old patriarch fish is feeding with a quiet metronomic cadence. There is usually time for only one or two fish before it either gets too dark, or the rise peters out, or, more commonly, the entire pool is disturbed by the fight of the hooked fish. This, too, is an added attraction, a further distillation of the experience.

When the conditions conspire in your favour, and if you champion a sniper's instead of a shotgun approach — one good cast over many hopeful ones — the evening mayfly hatch on the Motueka is dry-fly-fishing at its best.

On this day, just thinking of the promised spectacle during the drive from Picton was enough to make my heart glow with anticipation and hope, the breath quicken and the hands sweat lightly against the steering wheel. By the time I arrived at my chosen pool I had a mild case of trout fever, the kind that makes you fumble with knots and drop tiny flies, and repeatedly fail to find the eye of the hook with the sharp end of the tippet because your hands tremble ever so slightly. Getting ready, I tried not to hurry, taking deep breaths and repeating an old Latin precept so useful in fly-fishing: *Festina lente*. Make haste slowly.

Over the tail of the pool not a whisper of wind ruffled the weightless flutter of Blue Dun mayflies as they broke away from the surface. A few smaller fish were already splashing in the feed line, a sure prelude to a full-on evening rise. I had come just at the right time. Everything was perfect.

Too perfect.

Presently, a nose of a red twin-cab 4x4 ute appeared in the access driveway, paused for a moment, its driver taking in the scene, then unceremoniously jolting and crunching his way across the rocky riverbank, going too fast, as if angry that the bank was so uneven, and that by driving fast against it he could flatten it. He came to a halt directly between me and the river, the truck's front wheels almost reaching the waterline. The engine stopped, the door flung open and a pear-shaped man emerged dressed in gumboots, track pants and dirty work shirt tightly stretched over his beer belly.

He appeared to be avoiding looking at me, as if I were not there, halfway into my waders, with the rod rigged and resting against the snorkel of my camper. He walked around to the back of his truck and in the loose junk scattered around the ute's tray began rummaging for his fishing gear. This did not take him long, as in the next moment he was splashing through the shallows and towards the rising trout. The trout which I had been anticipating for the past few hours, and whose every rise added an extra beat to my own heart rate.

What do you do? Confront the dude? This can be a no-win scenario. You fight, you're a fool; you walk away, you're a coward. The impossibility of avoiding other anglers on New Zealand rivers, and the unpleasant run-ins which such encounters can lead to, have now become so common that Fish & Game has produced double-sided signs that anglers can leave behind the windscreens of their parked cars. *Fishing upstream from here* (*downstream* on the reverse side). And on both sides: *I'm a friendly angler but not here for the company, so please respect my space*, or words to this effect.

Most often than not I've found that riverside confrontations are the result of one party's ignorance. Your weekend wa― his brand new Sage or your overseas tourist used to f to-elbow on stocked ponds genuinely may not unders you stalk wild brown trout you need room to move an― ―er to cover. They may not fathom that even walking the ri―er bank, without a single cast, can spook fish, and it can take hours if not days for them to come back and start feeding again; that water already covered that day is considered *second hand* and thus a waste of time to fish. Or that cutting in front of a trout hunter cat-footing the riverbank is likely to elicit an emotional outburst which makes

My first thoughts were to question the marital status of his parents, or perhaps the profession of his mother but, really, was it their fault that what they conceived half a century ago turned into an arrogant old grump?

the most severe case of road rage benign by comparison.

The thing to do was — always — to communicate, to enquire about the first-comer's intentions and then to respect them. This simple act often diffuses a potential confrontation, with the response likely to be along the lines of: 'I'll only fish to the next corner, the rest is all yours.' The result is sharing of a river, the sense of a silent brothers-in-rods kind of kinship, sometimes a few fresh tips or insights, even a new friendship.

Well, clearly, I wasn't about to make friends with Pear Man, but I felt I could not let the matter drop, either. There was an unacceptable 'this is my river so bugger off' kind of meanness to the way he barged into my riverine dream and shattered it. This was no innocent mistake or ignorance; this was a premeditated affront. A slap in the face. Something that caused your blood pressure to spike and made you think: 'Someone ought to teach this punk a lesson.'

I tied Mops to the tow bar on her long rope; Airedales are naturally too friendly to be ambassadors of vengeance. I left my rod where it was, leaning against the camper, so that it would not get in the way, then started walking towards the man. Beyond him I could see that among the splashy reckless rises there were now others, spare and measured, a clear sign that bigger fish were joining in the feast. There was a good twenty metres between me and Pear Man, so I had ample time to consider my opening gambit.

My first thoughts were to question the marital status of his parents, or perhaps the profession of his mother but, really, was it their fault that what they conceived half a century ago turned into an arrogant old grump? I wanted to ask him if perhaps his digestive tract was upside down, with its two distinct ends unfortunately swapped around, or if his brain was made not of grey matter but of a different, foul-smelling substance, manure-like. In my agitated state, I was not short of possible expletives, but I quickly ran out of distance and time to choose one.

'Hope I'm not interrupting, mate,' I said and he grunted something without looking back. He stood ankle-deep in the water still fiddling with his gear, which I could not see.

His grunted reply was predictable: something rhyming with 'muck', slurred into an 'off', and followed by another short word I did not quite catch. And maybe just as well. Pear Man was a ripe subject for some talented anger-management consultant, though right now I felt I could use the help of one, too. There was no backing out, however. Not now.

'Don't know if you noticed, but something fell off your truck when you were bouncing over those river rocks,' I ploughed on.

'Eh?' he turned to me in mild surprise. His face was slack and jowly, red and unshaven, but his mouth seemed set in a permanent grimace of distaste, as if he didn't like the smell of something under his very nose. His small, shifty eyes regarded me with suspicion, then turned towards the riverbank, retracing the way he came.

'It was kind of small, but I think it was important,' I went on.

'Wha' was tha'?' he finally spoke, looking back to me.

Perfect presentation, I thought, now for the take.

'Your angling etiquette, mate. Didn't you see me getting ready to fish?'

He turned away and back to the river with a horrible huffing sound and only then I saw his gear. It wasn't just the sloppy looks and the attitude. Pear Man really was a *plonker*. In his hands he held a telescopic spinning rod fitted with an egg-beater reel, and at the tip of the rod there dangled a silvery ticer he was about to start lobbing at the rising fish.

Now, I've got nothing against spin-fishing. I own an Abu bait-casting rod, for salmon, sea river mouths, and times when the water is just too big to fly-fish it well. The rod comes with an open-face Ambassador 6600 C4 reel which is so beautifully engineered I often find myself fondling it, and turning its handles dreamily, and the sensation is pleasantly soothing, almost contemplative, as if the thing was some sort of high-tech prayer mill. But to spin-fish for trout rising to mayfly duns just bigger than mosquitoes? He might as well have been throwing stones at the fish, which, in effect, was what he was doing.

My anger and indignation instantly evaporated. This was ignorance, after all, just thickly disguised by a layer of boorishness, and I had a premonition that his antics would be worth watching for their high entertainment value. Just how high I could have had no idea.

Pear Man lobbed out a cast, and — *plonk!* — it landed right in the feed line. I had to give him credit for accuracy, though, to be honest, if he was to get one of those rising fish he'd have to stun it with that ticer then immediately hook it with the treble hook attached to it. It was like watching someone extinguishing candles in a shooting gallery. Wherever the ticer landed, the rises instantly ceased.

I stood on the bank and watched — and Pear Man knew that I was — and maybe the pressure of it all was too much for his nerves, for he misjudged one of his casts and sent it right into the branches of the willow overhanging the far side. The reel snapped into its 'retrieve' mode, and the heavy nylon twanged across the river. Pear Man yanked it a few times, causing willow leaves to snow down into the water, but the treble hook held fast. He grasped the reel with one hand and started putting his weight into the pull, and I took a few precautionary steps away from the river.

In my late teens I used to spin-fish for pike in the lakes of north-eastern Poland. The lakes were weedy, and so it was easy to get snagged. The matron of the house I stayed in worked at the local ambulance station, and, as a warning to a young angler, she recounted how she could always tell when the fishing season started because on the doorstep of the emergency room men would appear, rods in hands, treble-hook lures dangling from various parts of their facial anatomy — ears, lips, cheeks, eyebrows — like some form of bizarre exotic piercing, the nylon often still uncut, running through the rod's guide-rings to the reel. Pulling at a lure snagged in weeds is akin to shooting an arrow back at yourself, the arrow's tip armed with a treble hook.

Maybe Pear Man didn't know that, and in any case, the anger he had brought with him to the river probably did not help. He yanked harder and harder, and watching this I began to hope his line would snap first before he'd have a chance to hurt himself. But what must have been shark-gauge nylon did not snap.

Instead, the willow branch finally gave and the lure shot back across the river. It missed Pear Man but glanced a vicious ricochet off the river rock, and reflexively, at the sound of it, he dropped his rod and cowered, throwing up both his arms to protect his face from the blow that did not come.

I tried to keep a straight face, but it was hard. Pear Man's cheeks went two shades redder as he furiously reeled in all the loose line.

'Did it ever occur to you that the winding action of an egg-beater reel looks faintly, well, masturbatory?' I wanted to say, but thought better of it.

Besides, the plonker was already throwing his gear in the back of the ute, sliding into the driver's seat and, if not quite laying a yelp of rubber on the rocks — the riverbed was too rough for that — then driving off even faster than he came in, the ute bucking mercilessly against the rocks.

When he reached the road he stopped briefly, whether to pick up his angling etiquette or just to disengage the hubs I shall never know.

I turned back to the river. Along the feed line under the willows the trout were rising again, and some of the dimple rings were soft and light like child's kisses. I looked up into the fading sky and smiled to myself. The dream was not shattered, just foreshortened. There was another half an hour of twilight left.

I wish that, the way secret manuscripts ought to, the thing arrived on our laps bound in Moroccan leather, dusty and smelling of Muscilin and old fly-tying capes. That it was penned in permanent ink, calligraphied almost, in a neat and precise hand, filled with hand-drawn maps dotted with X spots and question marks, and with watercolour sketches instead of snapshots. Alas, no, it came in a much more contemporary and prosaic fashion, by email and as a spreadsheet file. Nevertheless, it had Gazza and me drooling with anticipation, because what it contained was priceless, so never mind the banal form and packaging.

For over ten years, a certain European-born fly-fishing guide had fished and worked the north-western quarter of the South Island, especially around the Reefton area, which is about as good a headwaters fishery as you'll find anywhere in the world; some say the best. The rivers here are known to contain a disproportionately large number of trophy brown trout, which are fished for daily, and, as the season progresses, become impossibly hard to catch. Occasionally — just often enough to keep the legend alive — someone actually hooks one of these fish, but most visiting anglers come charged up and inspired by Reefton's reputation only to leave shortly afterwards, beaten up and empty-handed, the elusive trophy browns having got the better of their skills and patience, and sometimes their spirit as well.

A telling piece of local fly-fishing lore, repeated with relish and a wink, recounts how one day three guides fished three different beats on Larry's Creek. It was tough going, and when they met that night in a pub to wash it off, they did the maths and calculated that among the three of them their clients had fished to seventy-five sighted trout that day, all large heart-stopping brutes, for there seem to be no small fish here at all. Not one of these seventy-five fish was hooked.

It was in such a place — hard to fish, and harder still to guide — that the aforementioned European excelled, and he did so by making it his mission to understand the fish and the rivers better than anyone else. His knowledge was such that his clients could expect to catch double-figure fish from waters that had already been fished that day. So great did his confidence grow that he became the only guide I ever heard of who could honestly guarantee a trophy fish, if you put in the time and did not mind a fair bit of discomfort. How he arrived at this state of omniscience was documented in his fishing diary, which recorded his methodical approach to rivers, seasons and flies, along with the results of every single day's fishing — information that was now nicely tabulated in a spreadsheet file locked in Gazza's computer. The European had long since retired from guiding, and the diary was a parting and magnanimous gift from him, a map to a treasure hunt if we could but follow it.

Having seen the guide in action, I thought that putting his diary to the test would make a worthwhile summer project. Gazza was already living in Reefton, attracted by the area's reputation of fly-fishing's kingdom come. I drove south and inland to Reefton, parked the camper on the lawn next to his house, and we got ready for a siege.

Gazza is about as competent an outdoorsman as they come. He acquired his firearms licence at about the same age he got his driving permit, and he was already a fly-fisherman well before that. His father had been a deer culler in the Dart Valley in the 1960s, and one of Gazza's formative memories was being weather-bound in a small hut up the Hopkins River, with his old man reading aloud to him and his two brothers from Wilbur Smith's *When the Lion Feeds*, while their mother cooked flapjacks over the open flames of the stone fireplace.

One of his brothers went on to become a hunting guide, and Gazza himself had always supplemented his income by selling wild venison and possum skins, running trap lines after his regular day job. He cut his hunting teeth stalking the shy Stewart Island whitetail deer and this honed his skills to such a degree he'd

Madame X

deer-hair cicada winged

turned to bow hunting, since, as he told me, shooting a deer with a rifle was no longer enough of a challenge.

But though he ties neat, slim flies and makes no fuss about the number of fish he can usually catch, the Reefton browns had humbled even him. His first peck at the diaries was a sign of things to come. Easing himself into the local conditions, he picked the ex-guide's never-fail river and, buoyed with hope and insider's knowledge, put in a twelve-hour day. He did not touch a single fish.

Soon after my arrival, Gazza selected a top-secret diary entry, one about a tributary stream which ran for several kilometres as broken, braided and unstable water, and it was thus avoided by most anglers. According to the diary, this was a fortuitous oversight, because above the nondescript section there was a long stretch of stable water peopled with trophy trout. From an advance camp up the valley we bush-bashed for about four hours until we found that stretch, a staircase of crystal pools and riffles, log jams and cliffed banks.

'Oh, yes!' exclaimed Gazza, hastening his stride. 'Any moment now we should start seeing some of the big boys.'

But we didn't. The water was an embodiment of a fly-fishing dream — pristine, clear, remote and stable — but hiking from pool to pool, gazing into their green depths from the abundant high banks, we did not see a single fish. Not even a fingerling. We began to wonder if the secret diary was some kind of practical joke.

I had fished around Reefton before, and usually managed to eke out a fish here and there, but never with any degree of consistency. It was clearly not a place for casual drive-by fishing, though there

were always cars parked near any water accessible from the road.
This was, I guessed, where most of the tough-luck stories were
born. The fish found there were so habituated to anglers they did
not even spook. They simply continued to feed around all artificial
flies thrown at them. I had watched these roadside anglers, taking
it in shifts trying to catch the resident trout, and had a rather
highbrow opinion of them, with their naïve enthusiasm and
belief in eventual luck. But now, driving back from the outing to
the mystery creek, sore-footed and dog-tired, I found my scorn
and condescension considerably mellower. We, the backcountry
purists, armed with kilobytes of tips and tip-offs, hadn't done any
better than the roadside crowd.

We decided to give the diary one more honest chance to deliver
what we thought it so readily promised. We picked a location the
European guide considered his greatest favourite, a river to 'die
on' as he put it, but only once we were in the valley did I realise
that this description was something of a double entendre, applying
not just to the potential quality of the fishing but the difficulty of
the terrain as well.

We packed for four days and hiked in along a faint trail, losing
it at times, casting out for it through the thick beech forest,
navigating around wind-fallen trees and crumbling banks, Mops
running from Gazza to me and back again, connecting us like a
courier, lolling her tongue in happiness at what was the longest
dog walk of her life.

We set up a camp on a patch of sand and anchored the tent pegs
with river rocks. We had already seen our first fish, nymphing
vigorously just where you'd expect a fish to be: in a pocket of
slower water where a feed line ran into a large submerged boulder.
We watched it lift in that telltale sideways drift, gracefully sinuous
and confident, as it came up to take a passing dry, and it seemed
like a good omen for the entire trip. Or so we thought until the
fish spooked on the first cast. So did the next many fish, no matter
how carefully we approached them.

'I can't believe this,' Gazza huffed after another fish shied away
at the sight of his dry fly. 'We're on a remote backcountry river,
hard miles from anywhere, and the fish are more spooky than
those in town.'

The cause was obvious. On every patch of riverside sand we
could see footprints, fresh and some of them excitedly numerous,
clearly a sign that a battle between a human and a fish had taken
place there. Obviously, the secret of the die-for river was out
before we got hold of the diary.

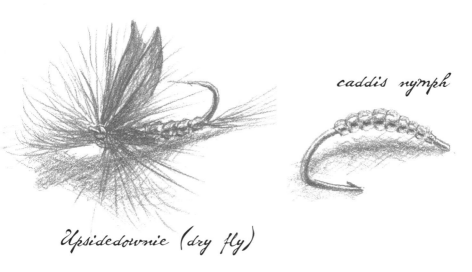

caddis nymph

Upsidedownie (dry fly)

Tom McGuane wrote that the pleasure of angling has nothing to do with success, yet the opposite is also true. The lack of success, or at least of an engaging interaction with a trout, can overshadow the best river day like too much cloud. Especially if you put in a supreme effort, walking for hours, hoping for fresh water and unmolested fish, and arrive to find the water second hand, the fish on tenterhooks. Especially if this happens several days in a row, and you develop an irrational conviction that no matter what you do and where you go this curse of being unable to touch a fish will follow you there. It is akin to the disappointment of the backcountry skier who, having hiked for miles in search of fresh deep snow, finds it trampled and soiled. Paradoxically, the solution to both quandaries is the same: a reset and a fresh start.

It rained hard all of the second night, as we knew from the forecast it would. There was no reason for concerns about safety, because the rivers here cope well with rain, even with the most intense downpours. They rarely discolour, though their tint darkens first to the colour of bourbon, then progressively to that of strong, black tea. They rage immediately after the rain, but when the weather clears you can watch their level drop faster than an outgoing ocean tide.

What a difference the rain made! It not only washed away all the footprints, but also apparently erased the fish's memory and their wariness of anglers. Bypassing the waters we had fished the previous day, we hiked for a couple of hours while the sun cleared the valley ahead of us and made the ostrich-egg river boulders steam in the heat.

We soon saw our first trout, and Gazza cast to it. The fish took the fly without hesitation, truly a miracle after the experiences of the past two days. It was my turn then, and I hooked the next fish with my first cast, too. Both trout were solid 6-pounders, 'nuggety', as Gazza would describe them, their bellies fat and white to match the bone-coloured riverbed, their upper halves camouflaged with a pattern of whisky-gold specks.

Gazza looked up and pointed to a rise in the tail of the next pool. He was already changing to a *Coloburiscus* emerger.

'That wasn't in the diary,' he said with glee.

'What? The difference the rain makes?'

He just shook his head. Maybe it was just as well it was not in the diary. We had relied on the darn thing as if it was a panacea to all our trout problems. But, finally, after all those miles and disappointments, we were on the money, and we would be for the rest of the day, until the light ran out and we had to slog back to the camp in semi-darkness.

We did not encounter any of the European's famous doubles, though once or twice Gazza reached for his digital scales and weighed the net with fish in it, only to confirm that, too bad, it was just under the 10-lb mark.

Lying in the tent that night, with Mops stretched out at our feet and snoring in exhausted contentment, I thought how on this 'to die on' river something has died within me, too, and that it was as welcome and liberating as the shedding of old clothes that had become too tight.

I was free from the self-imposed tyranny of the diaries, free to be on my own treasure hunt, without trying to follow someone else's path and expertise. I don't know why, but we had latched on to the guide's notes as if they had answers and solutions to all that we wanted to know about trout around here. But they were just a string of riverside snapshots recorded by a competent fisherman a decade or so before. Nothing less, nothing more.

The diary was not the guide we had hoped it would be, and certainly not a short cut to trout. In the end, we had to figure it out ourselves, helped along with a little luck — though maybe you earn such luck by putting in the time and the mileage. In the end, we all keep our own diaries, written or not, and they are the ones that matter most.

In fly-fishing there are very few short cuts worth taking, and the beauty of our quest is that there are no lasting formulas, and all patterns eventually fall apart to be replaced by new ones, equally transient. All the science in the world cannot model the next day's fishing or assure that the magic we seek will happen, for that comes in its own time, and all we can do is to be there, prepared, ready to receive it.

In a garage studio on a cliff above the Ahaura River, east of Blackball, Johnny Groome stepped back from his easel and regarded the canvas with a critical eye. A heavily-timbered stag, trotting up an alpine game trail and pausing momentarily to glance over its massive shoulder, looked back at him from the unfinished painting with a mixture of curiosity and defiance.

'Enough work for today,' Johnny said, stabbing his brushes into a tin of turpentine. 'Let's go for a fish. I'll show you my best river in the world.'

I have come to see him about just that, my curiosity piqued by his book *Arnold Gold*, full of stories about large flies and amazing *Coloburiscus* hatches and a river that no one else seemed to care about. Years ago, during my exploratory forays to the West Coast, I looked at the Arnold but dismissed it after a cursory glance. It seemed too hard: intimidating fast water, so dark it was impossible to look into, all of it hemmed in and overhung with willows, with an impenetrable thicket of blackberries and brambles blocking all access like bales of barbed wire. I went on to Reefton instead, and this, Johnny was now telling me, was the mistake everyone made.

'There are three types of trout waters on the Coast,' he said as we drove down to the river. 'Your lowland waters like La Fontaine and all the spring creeks, your backcountry rock-and-boulder rivers that everyone goes for, and then you've got the Arnold which I prefer above all the rest.'

Unlike most other trout rivers on the Coast — all of them rain-fed and thus prone to frequent and at times cataclysmic floods — the Arnold flows out of a large lake — Lake Brunner — and is thus uncommonly stable. This is apparent when you turn over one of the stones that cobble the riverbed: black with algae and trailing tendrils of weeds, and absolutely teeming with aquatic insects. But blink and you miss most of them because the water-blaster current washes them away instantly.

'One time I set up a fine mesh sampling net and then moved a few stones upstream of it,' Johnny said. 'The net yielded over 1000 critters, mainly net-building caddis and *Coloburiscus* nymphs. I try not to do this too often because, really, the bottom here is so old, undisturbed and densely populated that when you pick up

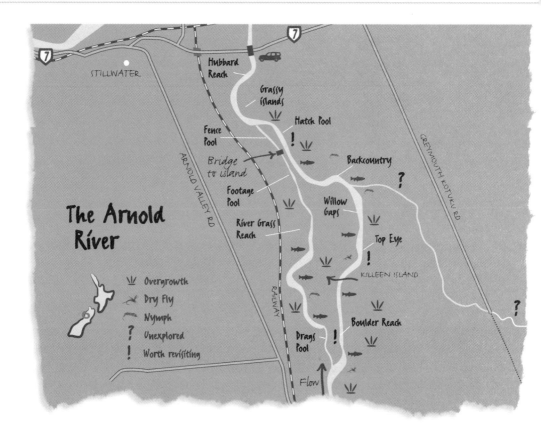

a stone you instantly want to put it back, feeling guilty about the havoc you've caused.'

It is this aquatic ecosystem — stable, long-established and unaffected by the heaviest of deluges — which makes the Arnold such a unique trout fishery. 'It is a haven for brown trout,' Johnny says. 'There is an overabundance of food here, unlimited shelter and almost no disturbance from anglers. The numbers of fish must be experienced to be believed. I have pulled out up to twenty good fish in a day from a patch of river the size of my kitchen. Based on my catch rates I'd guesstimate the numbers at 500 fish per kilometre, in places perhaps even more. This surely must be the highest density of trout anywhere in this country.'

None of it is immediately apparent as we walk upstream from the highway bridge and along the smaller channel of the main river called the Left Fork. If anything, my old impressions are reconfirmed. Absolutely no room to cast, arse-up wading territory and, worst of all, no sign of fish. The water is stained brown by the forest tannins, and it runs over a black bottom, frequently frothing into white water. No hope in hell to spot a trout, not even with a painter's visual acuity like Johnny's.

'What makes the Arnold such a Cinderella of a river is that it is a blind-fishing water in a region known for its sight-fishing,' he says. 'You try to spot fish here, you'll fail almost every time. But the trout are here, packed so tight you need to cover every square inch of the bottom.'

Easier said than done. I watch Johnny wade into the river at a small opening among the willows. The current instantly grabs his legs as if to take him down, but he makes confident if slow progress into the riffle with short shuffling steps, and starts to cast. His style of casting isn't something you would find in a book or demonstration video. He uses a mongrelised Spey flick which relies on the current to load the rod, because even a half backcast would result in a sure snag in the willows. But though his casts are not pretty, they are effective. Not three plops of a heavy nymph from starting to fish and Johnny is hooked up to a vigorous trout which tears downstream in a blur of gold.

There is a long and furious battle, a seesaw of give and take with neither man nor the fish giving in. Johnny, his legs trembling against the relentless current, feet seeking purchase on a riverbed as slippery as banana skins, is reluctant to follow downstream where the flow is even faster and deeper, and the trout, strong from a life spent in this muscular water, uses the current like a seasoned wakeboarder.

But clearly Johnny is an old hand at this. Slowly, he brings the fish in, guiding it through an obstacle course of sunken sticks and trailing branches, mindful of all the overhead line hazards. He releases the fish midstream, the barbless hook making it an easy pluck. 'Very impressive,' I yell out, but Johnny does not hear me. With another of those mongrel casts he is hooked into a second trout, almost in the same spot the first one came from.

This goes on for a while, fish after fish from barely a few square metres of fast water until Johnny motions me in to have a turn. My own rod is rigged up for dry fly — the inimitable *Coloburiscus*, no less — so I borrow his, clearly a proven set-up. It is a #7–8 weight walloper, with a long thick leader, a single bomb of a caddis nymph and no indicator. Casting with it feels like wielding a fireman's axe. But that's the easy part.

The current is so swift you have to start stripping the line even before the fly hits the water or you'll never catch up on its drift and feel the take. This makes for athletic and furiously fast fishing. I lob two dozen such casts, each time stripping the line like a madman but nothing happens.

'You musta caught them all,' I quip. 'There are no fish here any more.' Just as well I didn't bet on it. Johnny goes back in, and with a couple of those ugly casts of his, *bang!* — the axe of a rod is bent double again. Then again. Clearly, no shortage of fish, more a shortcoming in my angling skills.

'There is a bit of a knack to it,' Johnny says. 'But once you get it, you can confidently catch fish here any time. We regularly average ten to twenty fish every day. You can see what a tremendous resource the Arnold is. A backcountry river may take a few days to recover before it's worth fishing again. Here you can come every day of the year and always find fish.'

I'm hanging out for some dry-fly action, as Johnny had extolled the *Coloburiscus* hatches that used to be so consistent here you could fish them all day, seeing trout rising in nose-to-tail lines to mayflies so large you could just about hear their wings flapping as they came off the water. A few duns are fluttering about, rising in a slow and stately manner as befits their size, but we see no trout intercepting them.

Finally, ah, here's one! Johnny freezes, then slowly backs away from the water's edge, pointing to a trout that had just risen against our side of the bank. I get down on my knees, edge in closer and watch. The fish rises again and I have its position pinpointed. 'This is more like it,' I think to myself, 'here I am at home and confident again.'

The fish ignores the first two casts, Johnny's upside-down *Coloburiscus* imitation bouncing down the fast and narrow feed line, but the third time around there is a quick splash, then the familiar heaviness on the line as I lift the rod.

The fight is short as I muscle the fish in, not letting it run for fear of all the snags and branches. The trout is maybe 4 lbs, whisky gold and speckled like a gem. It vanishes the instant I release it, the water into which it returns black again and seemingly fishless.

I sit in the tall grass of the bank, silently relishing that inner glow that comes when you've worked for a fish long and hard, and then it all happened just perfectly — the sighting, the cast, the fight and release — like a miniature lifetime condensed into a few moments.

'This is where they want to put the artificial kayak course, a 300-metre concrete flume flushed at will to a dialled-in grade of white water,' Johnny says, making a wide, sweeping gesture that takes in the water into which my fish has just returned. 'And over there they plan a huge regulation pond. The new power station is supposed to go in further upstream.'

Hydrobiosis larvae

generic grub

Have I mentioned that Johnny Groome is pissed off? End-of-his-tether enough-is-enough kind of pissed off. The river on which he spent his childhood, which he has fished regularly and frequently over the past twenty-eight years, is about to be ruined — and the process is well advanced. In another hare-brained scheme of trading world-class trout for cheap megawatts a power company has been given a go-ahead to develop a hydro project on the river which would effectively spell the end of the Arnold ecosystem and its fishery as it is now.

Oddly enough, when the hydro scheme was first mooted all the traditional defenders of wild rivers showed little interest. Fish & Game ostensibly chose to focus on other, more important, river-saving battles, of which there are never any shortage. The Arnold's white-water kayakers opted for a pact with the devil and got a concrete slalom course as a sweetener. This left only Johnny willing to fight, and it also left him hopping mad because, as he sees it, no one knows the river as well as he does, and so no one else knows what is about to be lost.

Johnny Groome took the power company to court, and into a David-and-Goliath confrontation. But for all his passion and knowledge of riverine ecology, Johnny isn't cut out for the ruthlessness of a courtroom affray, and so the real-life Grisham characters of the corporate world made short work of bringing him down. They cited technicalities and befuddled the key issues in swathes of legalese. His case was trivialised, his papers misfiled, his arguments refuted by fishery scientists of dubious motives and unclear allegiances. Which is why Johnny wrote and self-published *Arnold Gold*, and why he is now filming a DVD to show the true nature of the river and its remarkable ecosystem.

'They all marginalise the Arnold, saying that the fish numbers are insignificant,' he says. 'Well, the point is that if you transplanted the river to England, say, among all those famous creeks and hallowed waters of fly-fishing, the Arnold would overshadow them all.

'The water clarity is low here, and so any drift-dive fish count gives a seriously false reading. For a start, most of the time you're in white water, trying not to drown or get strained against trees and snags. Then, most of the fish will be gone before you can get close enough to see and count them. I know this because I've tried to film them under water, and it's impossible. The visibility is only about two metres, so you can't see the fish at all. But you can catch them.' Watching Johnny do just that, I have no doubt his river holds an enormous quantity of fish.

Come and fish the Arnold. Johnny Groome would love you to. Unlike the rest of us, so secretive about our rivers, he wants everyone to know about his favourite water, because this may be the only way he can protect it from ruin.

Most of us choose our home rivers but in rare cases it is the river that does the choosing. It seems to me that the Arnold could not have chosen a more devout defender.

On the wall of 'Inky' McLellan's home in Westport there is a plaque bestowed upon him by the XII International Plecoptera Symposium in Lausanne, Switzerland. I'm sure you know what Plecoptera are, but let me remind you: from *pleikein* ('braided') and *ptera* ('wing') the word denotes an order of stoneflies, common trout food.

If you're like me, entomologically handicapped when it comes to stoneflies, you probably also have in your fly box a good selection of their supposed imitations, big, leggy and unsinkable, probably acquired hurriedly on one of those 'just in case' whims during a tackle-shopping spree.

None of my dozen or so elaborate stonefly patterns had ever got wet, partly as I innately mistrust nymphs that won't sink, but also because where I usually fish — in the lower half of the South Island — we use #16s and #18s, and to fish with a nymph half the length of your thumb seems, well, a bit crude.

But I was in Reefton, and this was apparently stonefly country. So when the rain set in for a couple of days I drove to Westport to see a man about a stonefly.

When I got to Inky's the rain was hosing the house like a water blaster. Inky ushered me into his office, a dimly lit room darkened further by curtains — a fitting ambience for what must be one of the largest stonefly morgues on the planet. Against the walls there were entire chests of drawers, each with a perforated bottom, holding hundreds upon hundreds of glass vials, neatly labelled and containing stoneflies sunk in clear preserving liquid. It seemed that what Inky didn't know about the stoneflies, science had most likely not yet discovered or did not much care about.

'These have just come from Patagonia for identification,' Inky said, showing me an addition to his collection, more glass vials in a wooden box. 'The University of Utah sent them. Many are probably new species.'

Inky found his way into plecopterology through fly-fishing. A Westport schoolteacher in the 1950s, he was undoubtedly one of the first fly-fishermen to explore the major West Coast rivers: the Mokihinui and the Karamea, and the host of tributaries in the Buller catchment, including many rivers around Reefton. He still talks about them the way you'd describe a familiar neighbourhood, right down to individual corners, pools, rocks and runs, and his fifty-four years of meticulous fly-fishing diaries are a testimony to some serious time in the backcountry.

During his years of stalking trout and boning up on streamside entomology, he realised that while a great deal of work had been done on mayflies and caddises, virtually nothing was known about the classification and distribution of stoneflies. Thus he found his vocation, and his own fly-fishing has never been the same since.

'Look at this brute,' Inky said, passing me a vial with a prized specimen. '*Zelandoperla denticulata*'. I found 'im in Jacksons Bay.' It was nothing like the dandies in my fly box. Inky pulled out a larger-than-life drawing, a pencil portrait of the creature, and it looked like something you'd expect to crawl out of the pub at the wee hours of the morning.

For more than half a century, Inky has pursued both trout and stoneflies, and the latter has led him to stints at the Max Planck Institute of Limnology (freshwater science) in Germany, the editorial board of Perla, the periodical of the International Plecoptera Society, to cataloguing and systematising Australian stoneflies (191 species), then New Zealand ones as well (104 and counting — see www.stoneflies.org.nz). Based on all this work, I asked, was there a quantum of streamside wisdom that he'd care to impart to us, plecopterology innocents but keen fly anglers nonetheless?

'You have to remember that not all stoneflies are aquatic,' he said. 'There are many that live nowhere near bodies of water. Also, keep in mind that stoneflies are an important, but very small, part of a trout's diet. You could ignore them completely.'

'Why didn't *you*?' I asked.

'Well,' he smiled. 'There was this one big and beautiful trout up the Nile River. That is the Nile down the coast from here, not in Egypt. When I caught him, he had in his stomach nothing but stoneflies. So you never know. Best be prepared.'

Of course. Just in case.

When it comes to flies, I'm a strong believer in simplicity and that the answer to that all-important question — 'What are they feeding on today?' — is usually the same: accuracy. A dozen well-chosen patterns, in different sizes of course, and of varying weight when it comes to the nymphs, will probably catch most of the catchable fish. It seems that New Zealand trout, like the anglers that pursue them, are relatively unsophisticated opportunists.

Thus I was delighted to find that Inky's lifetime study of stoneflies translated into one #10 pattern, which needed to be tied in two variations, green and brown, with the brown being far more common. 'You can fish them with confidence, at least wherever the water is clean,' he said. (All stoneflies are pollution intolerant, and their presence is an indicator of good to excellent water quality.)

'There is no need for anything fancy,' Inky went on. 'Keep the patterns simple, the more generic the better, and keep them heavy. There are stoneflies in every part of the country. If there ever was a land of stoneflies New Zealand is it.

I made a mental note to tie some in my camper, with so much tungsten they'd strike sparks off the riverside boulders if I ever let my backcast drop. Then I began to say my goodbyes.

At eighty-four, Inky doesn't fish much any more. Stairs give him trouble, let alone riverbed rocks. He still likes to go and cast a streamer if the riverbank is grassy and flat enough for his hips. But he continues to study his stoneflies — identifying and cataloguing them, drawing intricate sketches of the creatures that'd make fearsome villains in any sci-fi cartoon. This is the next best thing to being on the river again.

March

OUTSIDE ARUNDEL, NORTH OF GERALDINE, by the caissons of an old highway bridge, I stood staring into the steel-blue waters of the Rangitata River, cupped hands shading my eyes against the glare and the dust-blasting nor'westerly wind. The swift current, coursing over white boulders, belied the water's depth and blurred the riverbed. Yet here, hard against the rounded stones and nosing upstream, was where they should have been — if they were here at all. I strained my eyes, as if forcing them into a feat of X-ray vision so they might discern the torpedo-shaped quicksilver bodies quivering in the current. But nothing moved at odds with the river's flux, and the effort and the wind made my eyes tear up and blur.

It was early March, and a rumour had crackled down the Canterbury river telegraph, raising hopes, sparking excitement. Since long before daybreak we had stood, a line of a dozen or so men and women in waders, hip-deep in the river, swinging fishing

foam wing case emerger

rods with the vehemence of tennis players serving for match point, lobbing lures across the current.

The salmon were running again! As if by magic, they had materialised from the ocean and congregated at river mouths, as they had done every summer for over a century. From there, propelled by the urgency of hormones and the inevitability of fast-approaching death, they surged upstream in waves. They raced across gravel shallows, rasping their fat silver bellies into open wounds. They leaped up staircase rapids, then lay doggo in deep pools, resting before making another upstream dash.

Theirs was a one-way journey on a final tank of fuel, a race against time and fatigue. Their stomachs were already defunct and beginning to shrink, so the offerings we cast across their path held no allure for them. Only if the flashing, twirling piece of metal or obnoxiously colourful finger-long fly passed in front of their very snouts; only then *might* they snap at it, out of pure aggression, not hunger.

Not today, however. Not yesterday, not the day before. If the fish had passed this way, they had done it safely. One by one, muttering about fishing being 'a waste of time' and threatening to 'stay in bed in the future', the anglers reeled in their lines and returned to their cars, camper vans and caravans. They walked with the stooped gait of the defeated, heading home empty-handed for the umpteenth time. For a while I was alone in the slate-coloured landscape, in wind that could rip the doors off a car, wondering why, against all reason, odds and comfort, my mind was already

CDC emerger

Deleatidium emerger

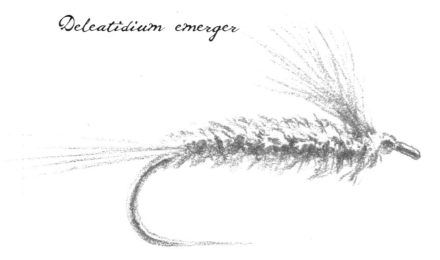

short-circuiting the rest of the day and racing ahead to tomorrow, the next daybreak, when I would again take my place in the line of anglers, hoping for the miracle of salmon.

My long-time riverside companion, a retired and itinerant Frenchman, Marc Hertault, was the primary reason for this madness. Monsieur Hertault lives the life of our dreams. Every day for six months he fly-fishes a New Zealand river between Taupo and Gore. For the other six months he does the same thing in North America.

A courteous gentleman who wears weathered clothes that look like discards from the Foreign Legion, M. Hertault is one of the happiest people I know. He lives in Spartan simplicity and has turned fly-fishing into both a scientific pursuit and a spiritual discipline. Above all, he is a walking anthology of stories about the incredible horsepower of *les saumons*, as he calls them. Many times, as we have lunched on a riverbank or bobbed in a dinghy on Lake Taupo, he has recounted how, having hooked a large salmon, he had to run — RUN! — several hundred metres downriver, holding his hyperbolically bent rod high above his head, hotfooting over boulders and driftwood. Not an easy feat for a septuagenarian wearing chest waders.

His tales come mainly from Quebec, British Columbia and Alaska. '*Ah, les saumons du Canada!*' he'd exclaim, theatrically sucking in a mouthful of air. 'Strong! Mean! Unstoppable!'

Then he'd launch into an impassioned recollection of yet another encounter with this greatest, noblest game fish on earth. I'd rarely get a word in, and when I did he'd say dismissively, 'Trout, yes, they're fun, but you haven't lived, *jeune homme*, until you catch a salmon. *Et les saumons du Canada* . . . ' And on it went, mercilessly. And so I fashioned a ploy to get my own back. You see, for all his angling expertise, M. Hertault was unaware that there are salmon in New Zealand as well.

Had the European settlers of New Zealand, who saw the country as an ecological *tabula rasa*, had their way, salmon would be as plentiful as sheep. As it turned out, the very fact salmon are here at all is a minor miracle.

All salmon are northern-hemisphere fish, originating from either the Pacific or Atlantic coasts. Pacific salmon are numerous, varied and known by a multitude of names, although ichthyologists distinguish only five main species: chinook (also known as king salmon, tyee, spring salmon or quinnat), coho, chum, sockeye and pink, or humpback, salmon. There are also a few lesser-known species, such as the Japanese cherry salmon and the Siberian taimen, a solitary and long-lived salmonid and one of the largest freshwater fish on earth (the heaviest verified specimen weighed 109 kg).

A breed apart is the Atlantic salmon, its original native range extending from the east coast of North America to Western Europe. Unlike Pacific salmon, the Atlantics do not always die after spawning and may breed several times during their lives. The Romans treasured this fish, and, having watched it swim past seemingly impassable river obstacles — salmon can propel themselves up three-metre-high waterfalls — they called it *salmo*, the leaper. In the British Isles the species attained an almost aristocratic status, and in 1215 the Magna Carta decreed that its habitat be protected and its passage unobstructed for all time. To colonists, *Salmo salar*, the Atlantic salmon, was the fish of choice for introduction to New Zealand.

At first, imported smolts — young salmon — were poured haphazardly into any river which took the colonists' fancy, whereupon they promptly disappeared, never to be seen again. A more methodical approach was deemed necessary, and the man chosen to run the enterprise was Lake Falconer Ayson, a Dunedin Scot whose self-taught expertise in raising hatchery trout had landed him the position of Chief Inspector of Fisheries in 1899.

With both brown and rainbow trout firmly established in New Zealand, Ayson set off to Europe and North America to research the Atlantic salmon and its habitat and to source the best breeding stock. He returned home with a firm idea that the best place for the fish would be the Waiau River, in Southland, as its temperature, flow and watershed most closely matched the salmon's northern-hemisphere habitat.

Ayson set about building a hatchery on the Upukerora River, an ideal spawning ground which connects with the Waiau via Lake Te Anau. Year after year he released millions of *Salmo salar* fry into the waterways.

But something was not right. The fish either vanished or became voluntarily land-locked. Only a moderate run (1000–2000 fish in 1930) established itself in the Upukerora, and since these salmon did not go out to sea, and so failed to take advantage of the rich food resources there, they remained relatively small — mere miniatures of the fish Ayson envisaged. Perhaps the water wasn't cold enough in the Waiau, Bob McDowall speculated, or maybe the fishes' navigational sense, tuned to northern-hemisphere magnetic coordinates, failed down under. Whatever the reason, the Atlantic salmon failed to establish a sea-going — or at least sea-returning — population.

One large Atlantic salmon, however, caught in fishing nets off the coast of Oamaru in 1897, was proof that the fish could indeed survive in New Zealand waters. The incident helped keep the salmon dream alive, and over the following century anglers persisted in their attempts to introduce the fish. In 1960, a shipment of ova from Scotland was released into the Waiau, and the following year brood stock from the Baltic was tried. As recently as 1983 there was a proposal to liberate Atlantic salmon into the Buller River, but the release never eventuated. Today, a remnant stock of Atlantic salmon is confined to the Lake Te Anau catchment, where, like the dream of the unstoppable leaper flashing up the South Island's picture-perfect rivers, the fish is considered close to extinction.

Fortunately for today's anglers, Lake Ayson's salmon interests were not restricted to the Atlantic species. At the same time as he was introducing *Salmo* fry to the Upukerora, he was hatching a parallel project on the Hakataramea River, a tributary of the Waitaki. The idea was the same: a single-point, large-scale, long-term release, but of another salmonid species. Here he would try chinook, the largest of all Pacific salmon, capable of tipping the scales at 50 kg.

Ayson planned his campaign meticulously. He selected a relatively coastal strain of chinook from California's Sacramento River — one that he hoped would not get lost at sea — and he chose the Waitaki River in the belief that the Southland Current, sweeping up the South Island's east coast, would disperse the fish northwards into other big rivers.

The venture was an immediate success. Between 1901 and 1907, Ayson made five importations and releases of fry, fingerlings and juveniles, and by 1907 the chinooks (which would become known here as quinnat, another native American name for this species) were already coming back to spawn. Ayson was delighted. Some of the fish weighed up to 11 kg. He stripped them of ova to produce yet more fish, and so reared the first generation of truly New Zealand salmon.

By 1911–12, quinnat had colonised the Waitaki River system and were spawning as far inland as the Ohau, Pukaki and Tekapo Rivers. Bolstered by additional releases, they had also spread out along the coast, both north and south, and were soon fully established in all available habitats. Before a series of hydro dams on the Clutha River blocked their passage, quinnat would swim up the entire length of the river, traverse Lake Wanaka, proceed up the Makarora and spawn in rivers such as the Wilkin and Young, in the heart of the Southern Alps. With the possible exception of Chile, where coho and chinook — escapees from sea-cage farms — may have established self-sustaining runs, New Zealand is the only country in the world where salmon have successfully acclimatised outside their natural range.

Although there are now small though increasing salmon runs along the West Coast — notably into lakes Mapourika and Paringa — and stray fish have been caught as far north as Taranaki, it is

> *Compared to fly-fishing for trout, catching a quinnat is supposed to be a relatively uncomplicated affair, involving rudimentary gear, basic skills and a fair dose of good fortune.*

Canterbury, with its glacier-fed rivers cutting wide braided courses across the checkerboard of the Canterbury Plains, which remains the quinnat centre of New Zealand.

As I drove along the coastal highway that early March, it was apparent just how much a Canterbury tradition salmon fishing had become. The mouths of the Rakaia and the Rangitata had spawned suburbs of salmon cribs, and any time during the fishing season, especially at daybreak, a forest of swaying rods could be seen where river meets surf. Fish & Game's statistics show that salmon fishing is by far the most popular form of angling in the South Island. During the record 1994–95 season, Canterbury's salmon rivers saw approximately 207,000 angler days. That's like the combined population of Nelson and Wellington going fishing on a single day.

Compared to fly-fishing for trout, catching a quinnat is supposed to be a relatively uncomplicated affair, involving rudimentary gear, basic skills and a fair dose of good fortune. But what it lacks in angling finesse, salmon fishing makes up for in the size and taste of the prize. A good fish can weigh 10–15 kg, which, at shop prices, converts into $200–300-worth of gourmet eating.

'Each cast is a lucky dip,' a guy named Gordon told me near the Waimakariri mouth, as he was stowing his rod and changing his clothes, ready to go off to work. No fish today, he said, but when the salmon were running it was worth calling a sickie.

On the Waimakariri I saw more women fishing than I had ever encountered on trout rivers. There were regular pull-in areas along the riverbanks, time-worn like West Coast whitebaiting possies, each with a car — doors open, radio crooning — sometimes with the family Lab tied to the tow bar, and a cardboard box with sandwiches and Thermos showing in the boot. Only metres away, poised like herons, Mr and Mrs Angler were casting their lures with a motion that resembled upside-down golf swings. Plonk! The metal hit the water. There was a pause, then the slow twirling of a reel. Another cast. Plonk! Time passed pleasantly as the sun lifted out of the ocean. I saw many such snapshots of family riverside idylls. All that was missing was the fish.

Maybe it was just my luck, but everywhere I went there were the same long faces, bitten lips and shaking heads, the same disbelief. What had gone wrong with the river telegraph? Where were the fish? As fruitless days slipped by, it became increasingly clear that the fish hadn't shown up yet, or else they did so in such small numbers as to make the already chancy odds almost negligible.

Later, I read a report in a fishing magazine about one of the year's more successful anglers, who caught just eleven salmon. His statistics summed it all up: he calculated he averaged sixty-five hours of fishing time per salmon — roughly eighteen forty-hour weeks in total; more or less a full-time occupation over the season. His story reminded me of what a whitebaiter once told me on the West Coast: 'During the season you get most of your 'bait in two or three days. You just never know which two or three out of the hundred.'

A few years ago — before he contracted an extremely rare disease known as necrotising fasciitis, or galloping gangrene, while diving off Stewart Island, and lost part of both his legs and nearly his life — I had the good fortune of spin-fishing for salmon with Ross Millichamp. For a dozen years prior to our meeting, Ross had been living two lives. In one he was a salmon-fishing fanatic, author of a guidebook he called *Salmon Fever*, because chasing salmon, he said, was like being caught up in a gold rush. In the other he was regional manager of Fish & Game North Canterbury, dealing primarily with, you've guessed it, salmon and salmon anglers.

The day he took me out fishing I met him at dawn in a central Christchurch suburb as he readied his jetboat. Soon we were driving south for an escapade on the Rakaia River, his favourite. The amber-lit streets were still empty, although the traffic thickened as we approached the launching ramp. The season had been poor so far, but Ross seemed unfazed by what others perceived as a national calamity. 'You need to understand that salmon runs go through natural rise-and-fall cycles, with big variations from one year to the next,' he said. In an average year, some 37,000 quinnat return to the South Island's rivers to spawn. Around 10,000 enter the Rakaia, several thousand more head for each of the other big rivers — the Waimakariri (6000), the Rangitata (8000) and the Waitaki (8000) — and the remaining 5000 home in on smaller rivers like the Hurunui and Opihi.

In any given year the run can fluctuate between 10,000 and 75,000 fish, of which anglers catch about a third. In the Rakaia, the best and most popular river, the runs vary from 1500 to 22,000 fish.

'It's a bit like the stock exchange. You get bull and bear markets,' Ross said. In the mid-1990s, the fishery was booming, and both the size and the number of salmon were the best anyone could remember. The fishing peaked during the 1995–96 season and has since been in decline. There was a similar boom-and-bust cycle in the 1980s. 'We seem to be at the statistical rock bottom of a cycle,' he said. 'In Nature, as in the economy, market corrections are inevitable. It may be just a case of riding out the bear and waiting for the bull to charge in again.'

By then we were doing a little charging of our own: a white-knuckle ride to the first salmon pool. The current of the Rakaia is fierce, and to keep the jetboat on the plane Ross had to go fast, so the river unrolled ahead of us like a computer game, the many braids an endless multiple-choice test requiring instantaneous decisions. We slalomed around entire trees brought down by floods, powered up rapids and grated across gravel shallows. Sometimes, Ross told me later, a braid can simply run out in front of you, resulting in a spectacular high-speed beaching. This usually happened early in the season, when reflexes were still rusty from winter disuse.

'Jetboats were made for this,' he grinned, shouting over the roar of the engine as we careered out of a cul-de-sac. 'I wonder if Bill Hamilton would have invented the jetboat if it wasn't for salmon fishing.' It was an interesting thought. The self-taught farmer–engineer who, among other things, helped design and build the country's first ski tow, was born near Fairlie, in the heart of salmon country. His jet engines would revolutionise the world of boating. But before they blazed a wake up the Colorado, the Zaire, the Ganges and the Amazon, he tested them on the Waitaki, starting in 1953. The prototype boat was called *Quinnat*, followed by a larger, faster successor named *Chinook*.

The naming may have been coincidental, but it is biologically accurate: New Zealand quinnat never quite reach the size, or the horsepower, of the American chinook. The reason is that chinook usually spawn when they are between three and seven years old, while New Zealand quinnat reproduce at two to four, occasionally five.

Ross thought that differences in size between New Zealand and North American rivers might also be a factor. In the Yukon, for example, the fish must travel some 3000 km to reach the sea, while in the Rakaia the distance is only 100 km.

'American salmon rivers are long, but they also have large, sheltered estuaries, so the young fish can take their time travelling downstream,' he explained. 'Our rivers are short and fast, and they lack estuaries where the young salmon can ease into the saltwater life. New Zealand salmon are thrown into the deep end.'

As we weaved our way upstream, like hounds following a scent, Ross craned his neck to locate the likeliest places for salmon to rest — deep eddies or pools just downstream of major obstacles. His approach to fishing was businesslike. He drove the nose of the boat into the gravel and held it there with the engine revving against the current while I leapt out and dug the anchor into the bank.

Plonk! Plonk! Plonk! Ross tested the water with a few rapid casts, and then we were off again, looking for another pool. 'The more water you cover, the better your chances,' he said. 'If the fish are there, you usually get one within a few casts.'

Hours passed, measured out by the repetitive launching and anchoring of the boat and the sound of lures slapping the water. Of salmon there was no sign — not a splash, not a bite, nothing. The mountains grow taller as we travelled further and further inland, but the turquoise water seemed as lifeless as melted ice cubes. My enthusiasm sagged, though for Ross every cast seemed as important as the decisive ball of a Lotto draw. What will it be: all or nothing?

'I've got one!' he shouted. Sure enough, his reel was spinning like an electric whisk, his rod bent into a bow, pointing towards a salmon that was U-boating downstream. A battle ensued, but after the initial adrenalin rush this part was purely mechanical. With his heavy-duty tackle, Ross hauled the fish out of the river and dispatched it, *à la* Fred Flintstone, with a hefty rock.

The salmon was in superb condition, fat and the colour of stainless steel: a prime candidate for the backyard smoker. As I watched Ross wrap it in a jute sack, I recalled an old salmon hand telling me beside the Rangitata that the vast majority of fish are caught by only a handful of experts, while the other few thousand anglers simply make up the licence-sale statistics and occasionally

Brendan's willow grub

get lucky. Clearly, Ross was at the top of the first group and I was at the bottom of the second. But there had to be a way of crossing from one to the other, I reasoned. Through the jute, the fish's body felt firm and ice-cold, and I sensed my salmon fever firing up again.

If, in salmon fashion, you follow a river such as the Rakaia towards its source, along its interwoven braids and through its forcefully hewn gorge, you will notice that the water becomes progressively shallower and more transparent, until finally it splits into tendrils: spring-fed creeks as clear as kirsch and no wider than a single-lane country road, purling and meandering through open tussock valleys. Each of these feeder streams has a bed of finest gravel, with a unique chemical signature which the salmon recognise as the taste of home.

Scientists think it must be primarily the water's taste that guides salmon back to their birthplace. How else to explain this truly miraculous migratory feat? Imagine driving from Wellington to a specific small street in suburban Auckland, well away from the motorway system and which you know only from vague childhood memories. You are travelling without a map, and there are no road signs. What are your chances of success? By smell you might recognise that you were passing sulphurous Rotorua or the Kinleith paper mill at Tokoroa. Perhaps, if the windows are down, you might smell the sea as you approach Auckland. But is it the east coast, or have you taken the Manukau turn-off by mistake? Finally, and surely by a miracle, you arrive, and notice that many others have done so, too. It feels like a kindergarten reunion. There will be one last party, and then the end of it all.

There is perhaps no event in the natural world which inspires more rumination on life's ebb and flow than the salmon's journey from river to sea and back again. Baby salmon, known as alevins, hatch from eggs buried in the gravel by parents whose bodies have long since decomposed or been washed downstream. A yolk sack feeds them for the first two months of their lives, at which point they wriggle out of the gravel towards the light and into flowing water. By now they are 30–35 mm long and known as fry.

Feeding voraciously on insects, they continue to grow, being called fingerlings or parrs at 5–8 cm and smolts at 10–15 cm, and over several months make their way downstream. They pause near the river mouth until their bodies adjust to salt water, then enter the deep blue and vanish. What they do and where they go is anyone's guess. Except for some sketchy data from the sea-fishery by-catch, science still knows little about the salmon's life at sea in New Zealand waters.

What is known, however, is that the fish grow rapidly. A young salmon reaches around 2 kg after its first year at sea and 7 kg after its second. Fish that stay at sea for another year grow to around 12 kg. The predator toll is also known to be extremely high. Of some 5000 eggs laid in each spawning redd, perhaps only three or four salmon will survive to return to their birth stream.

When the survivors reappear at the entrance to their home river, they are in their prime and full of *élan vital*, driven by the 'must spawn' imperative. On their way upstream they are resolute and relentless. If they encounter an obstruction, they either surmount it or batter themselves to death against it. This extraordinary drive is surely one of the reasons anglers become so deeply hooked on salmon fishing. It is as if the salmon's determination and power are transferred up the line when anglers seek to stop the unstoppable. Monsieur Hertault's own travels are based around the salmon calendar; everything else is of secondary importance.

The few fish which successfully evade anglers and other obstacles reach their birthplace to face one last act of natural selection: competition for a mate. The females choose sites for their redds and, lying on their sides, dig hollows in the streambeds with sinuous, explosive movements of their tails, while the males fight for a chance and a place to reproduce.

By now the males have lost much of the flesh around their mouths and have developed a ferocious-looking hooked jaw known as a kype. The bodies of both males and females have changed in colour from silver to platinum-black and are literally falling apart. Where the skin has been damaged in fights or abraded by gravel, chunks of flesh are often missing. Tails and fins are ragged and worn, and snouts often dislocated.

After spawning, the females bury the fertilised eggs with layers of gravel, and then keep guard until, having run out of energy, they can no longer hold their own against the current and the water washes them downstream, leaving their lifeless, beat-up bodies stranded on gravel bars.

Their mission accomplished, all the adult fish die. Not one survives the ordeal. But as the spark of life trickles out of them, as the final twitch of muscles flaps a tail against the dry bank-side rocks, beneath the gravel of the rivers' tendril streams the miracle of new life is already stirring.

Considering the effort that salmon invest in the renewing of their kind, it is little wonder that river-keepers have tried to lend a helping hand, especially now that hydro developments on the Waitaki and Clutha Rivers have significantly reduced the availability of spawning habitat. The imprint of this assistance is still visible in the headwaters of the Rakaia. Along Double Hill Stream, a critical spawning water for the Rakaia, you can see the remains of early salmon-enhancement projects. The structures remind one of ancient aqueducts: timber weirs and rusting wheels that once controlled water levels, pools and canals. The main stream itself is a staircase of evenly spaced cascades and pools — a staircase made with shovels and hoes, the cascades mini-dams of carefully arranged stones, and the gravel raked as smooth as a driveway to make it all the more appealing to spawning salmon.

As well as having its spawning runs streamlined, the wild salmon population has benefited from large-scale top-ups courtesy of commercial salmon farming. It started as an experiment to turn New Zealand into a salmon-industry potentate, and though its fall-out is difficult to gauge, it certainly changed both the fishery and people's perceptions of it. The idea was elegant in its simplicity. Given that salmon return almost infallibly to the very streams where they were born, all that was necessary — in theory, at least — was to hatch large quantities of fry and release them into a suitable river. They would go out to sea, feed and grow without any supervision or care, then return as fat, free-range fish ready for harvest.

It was called ocean ranching, and it began in 1976. To start with, the ranchers faced stiff opposition from anglers, but the protesters were won over when they were guaranteed free angling access to the returning fish. In essence, the ranchers were paying the anglers a river toll in the form of all the fish the anglers could legally catch.

Early returns were dismal — only fifteen fish from the first liberation of nearly a million fry made it back up the home river — but the ranchers soon discovered that while releasing four- to six-month-old fish resulted in survival rates of well under one per cent, if they held the fish for longer, say up to a year, the returns went up to between five and seven per cent. (Two per cent was considered the minimum for commercial viability.)

Soon the rivers of Canterbury were awash with fry. In the mid-1980s, the peak of the ranching boom, more than six million young salmon were released every year at over twenty different locations. The most ambitious of these hatch-and-release operations was Tentburn, established in 1984 near the Rakaia River. Between 1984 and 1990, Tentburn released twenty-five million fish into the Rakaia. But despite initial optimism, ocean-ranching returns turned out to be consistently poor, with a survival rate not the expected five to seven per cent but more like 0.2–0.6 per cent. One by one the salmon businesses were forced to close shop, and by 1991 all large-scale releases had been abandoned. The ranchers realised that, with high rearing costs and unforeseen risks in river and the sea, it made better sense never to let the fish go. Thus salmon cage farming came into being, in Stewart Island's Big Glory Bay, in the Marlborough Sounds and in the Mackenzie Country hydro canals.

> *I chose a place on the upper Rakaia where I had seen locals fishing, and dug in for an offensive. It was a lovely spot to camp, in the foothills of the Alps, with squadrons of Canada geese winging their way overhead like V-shaped ticks of approval in the sky.*

So far I'd kept my pursuit of salmon secret from Monsieur Hertault, not wanting to expose myself and my quest to his ridicule, condescension or just plain ribbing. And a good thing I had, because catching salmon, much less bragging about it, was looking less and less likely. Trout, it seemed, could be figured out, at least to a certain degree. They could be understood and predicted, and even if you were right only some of the time, it was enough to catch them with reasonable consistency. But salmon remained a lottery further complicated by the fact that I did not just want to catch one; I wanted to do it with a fly rod.

I had quizzed various fishing guides for tips. One suggested that to maximise my chances I needed to find a good pool and camp nearby, so that every day I would be there first. It was no use fishing second-hand water, he said. Frank Schlosser, who had spent many years guiding out of Tekapo and regularly caught salmon on the fly in the Rangitata, suggested I use a Teeny line — a heavy shooting head with floating backing. Once laid out on the water, the line took on a horizontal L configuration, the long sinking section fishing deep where the salmon were supposed to be, while the floating portion allowed for precise mending and good long drifts.

I chose a place on the upper Rakaia where I had seen locals fishing, and dug in for an offensive. It was a lovely spot to camp, in the foothills of the Alps, with squadrons of Canada geese winging their way overhead like V-shaped ticks of approval in the sky.

When I rose before dawn there was a veneer of frost on the camper's windows, and I wriggled into my neoprene waders and crossed the river braids towards the main stream. Mops and I had the place to ourselves. I tied on a gaudy yellow fly — another friendly suggestion — and began to cast.

It was as uneventful as ever, the lifeless opaque water rushing by, slowly eroding enthusiasm and hope. The Teeny line is extremely heavy, and casting it is like throwing a grenade, but the fly must have reached the bottom because it snagged frequently among the rocks. I pulled the line up again and again to free the fly.

Until, one time, something pulled back. It was a dull, annoyed sort of tug, followed by a momentary pause — just long enough, I later thought, for the adrenal glands of salmon and angler to fire up simultaneously. In an instant, my reel whirred like a dentist's drill, and I quickly cupped it with my hand, fearing it might overrun and jam.

The line spooled out downstream. Salmon! It must be a salmon! Nothing else in the river could pull so hard.

'I have lived!' wrote Rudyard Kipling after landing a chinook on an Oregon river. 'The American continent may now sink under the sea, for I have taken the best that it yields, and the best was neither dollars, love, nor real estate.'

Now I have lived, too, I thought. Monsieur Hertault was going to hear about this, more than once. '*Ah, les saumons de Nouvelle-Zélande*,' I would say to him. 'Beasts! Monsters! Stronger than jetboats!'

Meanwhile, with rod held high like a banner of victory, I began to run down the river.

April

 THE FIRST TIME I MET MONSIEUR HERTAULT was on the 'urban' section of the Tauranga—Taupo River, near its outlet into Lake Taupo. There is a street of baches and holiday homes there, on the south bank of the river, and all the way along it the power lines are cobwebbed with the nylon and artificial flies of thousands of backcasts gone bad.

I had just hooked a good-size rainbow, which took the nymph, sank the indicator, then tore off towards the highway bridge, angling diagonally across the river as it did so, aiming no doubt for the thicket of blackberries that choked the opposite bank. Their barbed branches trailed in the water, spelling disaster if the trout got behind them.

The reel zizzed at a feverish pitch but as I fished a little too fine perhaps I feared putting much pressure on the trout, and so I hung on for all I dared until, miraculously, just short of the wall of blackberries, the fish stopped. Then it turned around and shot back straight at me.

This was even worse. By now I was into the backing, and though I stripped the line furiously I could not do it fast enough. It went slack, and I lost contact with the fish.

Through all this I was vaguely aware of an old man watching me from nearby on the bank. He wore the aforementioned Foreign Legion surplus, and a matching cap whose legend, I later read, was 'Le Specialiste'. He had a minimalist's fishing vest on — not the usual Christmas-tree type hung with gadgets — a mien of an expert and he held his fly rod as if it was a schoolmaster's cane. He regarded me studiously, but with visible disapproval, a grandparent watching his second-generation progeny doing something simple but screwing up more than it was reasonably expected for his age.

I was reeling in the slack when suddenly the line came alive again in my hands. The fish was still on! I short-roped it to the bank, not letting it get away again, and to my surprise the uniformed gentleman unclipped his net and landed the fish for me. In so doing he would also have had a quick peek at the fly the fish took. This, I was to learn later, was part of his information-gathering strategy.

The fish was fresh and solid, its crimson stripe, like an after-burn, running from its bullet-shaped head down the length of its body. But neither its fine condition, nor my lucky recovery, was to redeem me in the eyes of Le Specialiste.

'Vous avez fait, mon cher Monsieur, une erreur impardonable,' he declared with a tone of scorn and finality.

I had committed a capital offence, it seemed. The old man was so adamant and intense about it, it made me think of the bumper sticker I saw somewhere: Fly-fishing is not a matter of life and death. It's far more serious than that. I tried to explain, thinking that perhaps he had missed something of what had happened, but it was of no use. He would not listen, and waved away my excuses and 'buts' as if they were harmless but annoying insects, then launched into a detailed lecture on the importance of keeping a tight line while fighting a fish, all of it in patois-flavoured French.

In his eyes, I was obviously a fly-fishing neophyte. I needed help, and, fortunately for me, he just happened to be here to save me from my own ignorance.

This master–disciple assumption more or less set the tone for our friendship in the years that followed. Each time I opened my mouth he would lift his hand, indicating that what he was talking about was far too important to be interrupted. There was nothing for it but to listen to what he had to say. At close examination some of it had a lot of merit. Thus, never intending nor suspecting it at first, I became a sort of apprentice to Monsieur Le Specialiste. At least, I'm sure he always saw it this way.

Monsieur Hertault, or 'Grandpapa Truite', as I've come to call him, came to New Zealand almost by accident. In a French fly-fishing magazine, he read one of those swashbuckling tales of a heroic angler, a kind of trout d'Artagnan, slaying over 150 trophy rainbows in the upper Rangitikei. Hoping to better such deeds (if an amateur could come away with such tales imagine what a committed specialist could do), M. Hertault arrived in Auckland speaking not a word of English and, with the magazine article for his guide, commanded a bus ticket to Tauranga. The girl at the counter misheard him and, clairvoyantly perhaps, sold him a one-way to Turangi, where he should have been going in the first place.

In Turangi, by another fortuitous coincidence, Grandpa Trout bumped into Michel Dedual, the fisheries scientist and insatiable angler. This, by my rough calculations, would have been at least fifteen years ago, but since then Grandpa has considerably expanded his English vocabulary to include such important words as *fish*, *fly*, *good* and *no good*, a combination of which covers just about all of his day-to-day concerns, the important ones anyway. One thing which has not changed is that he always greets fellow anglers with a gallant lift of his cap, followed by a loud and unequivocal 'Bonjour, monsieur' which often makes the addressee instantly guilty about skipping those French lessons at school.

Grandpa's story, if you can get it out of him — and this is a slow process of gathering disparate fragments and fitting them together — is one that touches or inspires all who come in contact with him. It makes them re-examine their own lives, careers and priorities, with the result, more often than not, of spending inordinately more time on the rivers and among the trout.

For his entire working life, Grandpa Trout was a successful farm machinery dealer, a sole agent for a leading manufacturer. In the process, he made more money than he'd ever care to spend, but all to the detriment of his family life and health. Selling any kind of appliance to a French farmer was never a straight-to-the-point kind of transaction. It involved house visits, long discussions on all conceivable subjects and the ingestion of vast quantities of high-octane, home-made liquors for which the French countryside is so notorious.

Eventually, the doctors intervened and gave Grandpa Trout a 'do-or-die' ultimatum, in essence saying, 'If you want to go on living like this, then don't bother coming to see us again.' Propitiously, this coincided with Grandpa's sixtieth birthday, and that very day he began his own personal French revolution.

He axed all the excesses, guillotined *foie gras* and wine from his diet, and put himself on a strict fitness regimen. Then, looking for something that could occupy all of his senses, energy and time the way his business had, but without the collateral damage, he discovered fly-fishing.

He did not quite fall in love with it; rather, he decided that, of all pursuits, attractions and temptations life could offer a gentleman of leisure and means, fly-fishing would be the most satisfying and complete. He tested his theory by going on a short fishing vacation to Slovenia, and a few small trout and days among the rivers confirmed his decision. At this point, he knew almost nothing about fly-fishing, at least beyond the basics. But he soon would, for he studied and pursued it with tireless passion, as if he were catching up on a lifetime of neglect — which of course, he was. As I write this, Grandpa Trout is eighty, and if my calculations are correct, for the past twenty years he has averaged some 300 days a year on a river somewhere, half of it in French Canada, the rest of it in New Zealand.

Since my 'unpardonable error' on the TT, I've fished with Grandpa Trout every year, if only for a few days. Over the years, since his fish spotting wasn't good enough for his own high standards, he's come to specialise in dry fly, and has taken this style of fishing to an uncommonly refined level.

'If a fish is rising it is mine,' he would say with only a hint of bragging. And most of the time it was true.

He applied the same dedication to his fishing for Atlantic salmon in the rivers of Quebec's Gaspé Peninsula, to the point where he was catching so many fish the jealous locals dobbed him in to the licensing authorities. He was a non-resident fishing with a resident's permit, they said, and it was technically true, though they did not seem to have the same problem in the days when he was catching only two or three fish a season. Grandpa Trout refused to pay the non-resident river fee on principle, claiming he had lived in Quebec for fifteen or so summers, then told the vigilantes they did not know a thing about their own salmon, much less about how to catch it.

How he beamed every time he retold that story! He had plumbed the knowledge of Atlantic salmon to depths greater than anyone else he had ever met. He was catching fish when no one else, including guides, were touching a thing. Moreover, he had come face to face with the truth about salmon; he had seen it in the very eye of the great fish.

It happened like this. He had spotted a particularly large salmon in shallow water, and, as it is the custom in Quebec, had offered his proven streamer fly three times, all with perfect casts and drifts. The fish did not budge, at which point custom called for a fifteen-minute respite, as any further insistence was sure to spook the fish. Too excited to sit and wait, Grandpa Trout left his rod standing by the pool and went for a brisk walk, trying to get the quiver out of his breathing and the shaking out of his hands. Time dragged mercilessly, but Grandpa is a disciplined man, and he counted off each of the 900 seconds *comme il faut*.

Back at the pool, he changed flies and cast again, but still the salmon ignored him. It was the next cast that would prove to be the defining moment. As if waking from its slumbers, the great fish turned for the fly and began to drift downstream with it, the gaudy artificial an inch from its nose. Then, when it was level with Grandpa Trout, the fish rolled slowly on to its side, the silver body flashing like a shard of mirror, jagged and long. The salmon gazed at Grandpa, holding eye contact for what seemed a supernaturally long time, then leisurely swam back to its previous holding place and parked up there.

Grandpa knew better than to cast again. He did not quite drop to his knees, but he took off his cap, and sat there watching the great fish that gave him this near epiphany, this glimpse of the Truth in all things. When he was done, he picked up his rod and strolled down the forest track to where his mountain bike was stowed. He was humming to himself a wordless tune, punctuated with snorts of laughter, something I noticed he does often when on the river. He knew he had made a mistake: he should never have stared back at the fish, not into its eyes, anyway, for in that moment some wordless communication had passed between them, and this made the fish uncatchable. That was fine by him, though. Glimpses of Truth often come at a price.

It was months later that a professional deer hunter Rob Wilson told me something that put Grandpa Trout's story into sharper relief.

'When you hunt an animal, you must never look it in the eye,' he said. 'I don't quite know what it is, but it's undeniable. When the eyes of the hunter and the hunted connect there is an instant understanding of who is who, and who is about to do what. Camouflage and distance are irrelevant. From the moment of eye contact, no matter how brief, they *know*, and their bodies go into overdrive, turbo-charged by panic. Most often they bolt, at which point you can't really shoot them well.

'I know it sounds a bit esoteric but I've learnt it the expensive way, shooting deer from helicopters,' Rob went on. 'You can look at any part of them — the nose, ears or antlers — and there is no problem. But the moment you look deer in the eye they're gone, and the weirdest thing is that it does not even matter that you look at them through the scope of your rifle.'

Grandpa Trout comes to New Zealand every spring, and to those who know him well enough, his arrival is the sign that the season has begun in earnest. I usually fish with him somewhere in Southland because the style of fishing there suits his gentlemanly manners and routines, the mayfly hatches being the most consistent of anywhere I know, and the fish numbers having to be seen to be believed.

This April we fished the lower Mataura, and as usual I endured Grandpa's endless tirades on everything from the construction of a perfect dry-fly leader to the unquestionable superiority of a sparsely tied Blue Dun over a Parachute Adams. His season in New Zealand was coming to an end, but the mayfly action was so good it was hard to leave, and, in hindsight, it was a good thing we did not leave too early, because another near epiphany, a moment of truth in all things by way of trout, was coming our way.

We were fishing to quietly rising trout, catching most of what we could see. We stood a few metres apart at the tail of a large pool. It was still and sunny, and the willows were beginning to turn yellow. Peace, solitude and utter contentment ruled. But then it started.

As if some invisible hand were turning up the volume, the intensity of the rise went up from quiet, to intense, to mad, to beyond belief. Within minutes, dozens upon dozens of trout were breaking the surface all around us, not so much taking individual insects as dredging the surface with their mouths open, the way whale sharks sieve through a plankton bloom. They cut wakes like channels of clear water through the mat of mayflies that covered the surface, brown and thick.

Grandpa Trout put his rod to one side and watched, waist deep in the water and motionless like a tree, himself creating a clear-water wake to the drift of untold number of mayflies. He had a bemused smile on his face, lightly biting his lower lip, and his head moved imperceptibly from side to side.

'I have never seen anything like it,' he said.

The boil went on for about fifteen minutes and, needless to say, we did not catch a single fish during this time. You could say it was because there were too many natural flies in the water so that ours would go unnoticed. My guess is that we forgot to cast, hypnotised by the spectacle.

When the explosion of mayflies subsided, the remnant insects drifting down and out of sight, the cadence of the rise returned to normal. I cast to the nearest fish and hooked it instantly. Grandpa Trout, pulled out of his trance, acknowledged my fish.

'*Voilà, il y en a une qui s'est suicidée*' — here's one that wants to commit suicide,' he said, then corrected himself. '*Non, il y en a deux!*' No, there are two!'

I looked over and saw that he was hooked up, too, our two fish racing each other for the opposite bank, the reels singing in a half-decent harmony. His needed oiling, I thought, but said nothing, not wanting to provoke another sermon. By now I knew that it was best for the apprentice, willing or not, to keep his mouth shut and just distil the wisdom from the barrage of words that came his way.

Later, when I examined Grandpa's rod, I saw that the cork handle had a deep groove where his thumb always pressed. This was not ergonomic design but wear from thousands of casts. The oval guide eye of his reel had grooves in it too, cut into the metal by countless fish power-stripping the line. The reel may have sounded like a rusty eggbeater, but the ancient battle-scarred thing had every right to rattle and whine as it did.

On the way back to the car I heard Grandpa Trout hum to himself his tune of self-contentment, and I knew I'd miss it when he was gone, and would wait to hear it again next spring.

As we put away our rods he stopped me with all seriousness to impart another morsel of wisdom, his index finger pointing skyward, ready to forestall any interruptions.

'The most important thing,' he said, 'is to avoid eye contact with the fish.'

Towards the end of April I bought a small boat of my own, an inflatable tender made by Aakron, and christened it *Waka Foo-Foo*, reasoning that the name was a plausible description of a blow-up vessel in pidgin Polynesian. Rolled up, the boat fit snugly in the back of the camper, but inflated over its wooden floorboards it made a stable platform from which to cast and spot fish. I had quite a few locations in mind where such a craft would open new waters, inaccessible on foot, and for her maiden voyage I took her to one of them: Lake Moeraki, north of Haast.

From the air, the lake is a bead of tannin-coloured water set

> '*A man should think when he is fishing of all manner and shape of things, flowing as easily through his mind as the light stream among its rocks.*'
>
> RODERICK HAIG-BROWN

into the forest-clad hills, but on the ground its shoreline is all kahikatea swamp. The lake is an overflow of a namesake river that rapidly slows as it exits the mountains, like a hesitant pause before continuing on and losing itself in the Tasman Sea. I fished the upper Moeraki River before, too late in the season, and once tried to walk the spongy shoreline of the lake, getting myself thoroughly bogged. That time, jumping from one clump of grass to another, I came to a teetering halt on the edge of a hole filled with crystal water so deep that looking into it induced a sudden bout of vertigo. It was like the entrance to an underwater cave between me and the river mouth I wanted to reach, and there was no way around it. A small boat seemed the only sensible idea.

I inflated *Waka Foo-Foo* the night I arrived at the lakeshore camp, so that it would be ready to launch while the morning was still and fresh. At dawn I packed the dog, a dry bag with camping gear, and with the rod rigged up and ready against the transom I rowed towards the distant river mouth, cutting a stitch-line wake across the gun-metal surface. Odd how I never noticed that each oar stroke produced a pair of counter-rotating vortices.

At this hour the lake was smooth and moody, and wisps of fog hung over it, thin as skeins of candyfloss. The silence was broken only by the rhythm of my rowing, the dripping of water from the oars and the occasional honking of black swans as, ever vigilant, they warned each other of my approach. At the river mouth I beached the boat and tied it to a solid stump, then, with the dog at heel, started to look for trout. It wasn't long before I spotted one, lying deep under a tongue of faster current right against the bank. Often the easier the trout are to see the harder they are to surprise, and it always seems preferable to find fish in faster water. You can see them but they cannot see you, and for a hunter on the prowl this is a decisive advantage.

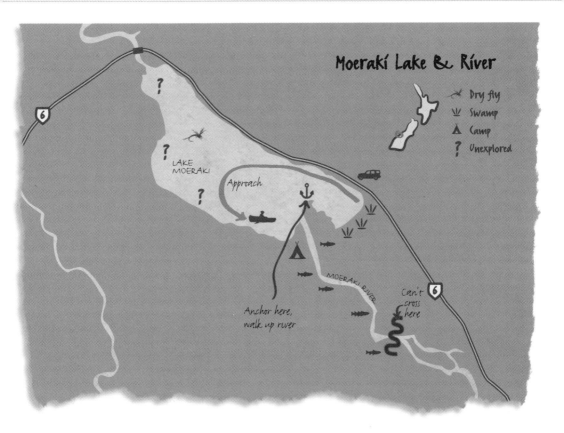

But was this really a fish? I looked and looked and could not tell for sure.

How many times have I stared into the water, trying to penetrate its shimmering, shifting flow, wondering about the shape underneath it. Was this a fish? 'It's in the right place, facing the right way,' I reasoned out loud, to myself and to the dog. 'It's definitely where a fish would lie, precisely on the colour change along the bottom, right where the fast and slow currents meet.'

A silent, cocked-head response from Mops, and more doubts from me. 'But is it a fish or just one of those fish-shaped brown weeds. Is that its tail that is moving, or is it just the current and shadows playing tricks with my eyes?'

The water was fast and broken, and no window of clear visibility drifted over the shape, to verify that what I was seeing was indeed a fish. But it was close enough, and certainly worth a cast. A couple of drifts and I was sure the fish had seen the fly. Did I just see him move to the side and take a look at it, or was it another optical illusion? More casts, different flies and, in-between, more screwing up of the eyes to penetrate the water, to touch with their penetrating gaze the dancing torpedo shape, to dispel the doubts.

Trout camouflage so well, their backs and flanks take on the colours and patterns of the bottom against which they lie. In one Southland creek I fish regularly, there is a type of rock the colour of wet brick that studs the bottom. It's not prevalent, just common enough to notice. The brown trout that live in this creek have gem-like brick-red dots on their golden skin, a precise match to the rock. In the main river they don't, but in this creek every fish I've caught has them. Not many dots, just enough to notice, and to marvel.

At times, while spotting fish and being unsure if your quarry is a trout or a trout-shaped stone, stick or weed, you look into and through the water so intently that when you close your eyes the scene does not change. Against the shut eyelids, you still see the moving water and the tantalising shape ghosting beneath its surface. Finally, convinced it is not a fish, you reel in and walk up close to it, and, sure enough, it is a piece of weed with plausible fins and tail, though sometimes, just often enough to sow more doubts for the future, the weed darts off into the deep. This is exactly what happened with my first fish on the Moeraki.

So you say to yourself, 'Never mind, it's such a beautiful piece of water,' and you keep walking, and staring into it, as if you were trying to drink the river with your eyes.

There was once a man who looked at trout in the very same way, and what he saw changed the world, or at least our perception of it. He was a genius inventor of the most unconventional kind, for he shunned all formal education and claimed that his knowledge came from observing and reflecting upon nature itself, its cycles, processes and the ways of its many beasts. In his time, the 1930s–50s, he was largely dismissed as a harmless nutter who communed with the fish — though only by those who did not know better.

Those who did know he was on to something good made every effort to extract from him his expertise, patents and inventions. Heinrich Himmler personally drafted him into the Secret Service, then made an offer he could hardly refuse: work with our elite research team or you'll be court-martialled and hanged. In the closing days of World War II, the Russians ransacked his Vienna apartment for research documents, then blew it up so that no one else could get what they might have overlooked. Later still, he was interned by American intelligence operatives. 'At the end of the war, I was confined for nearly a year by the American forces of occupation because of my knowledge of atomic energy production,' he wrote. 'After my release, under the threat of re-arrest, I was forbidden to take up again any research in the atomic energy field, although it would have been concerned with new aspects of this technology.'

Everyone it seemed, wanted a piece of what Viktor Schauberger knew, even if they did not know, or care, that it all started with him watching trout.

Schauberger, a man with shovel-blade beard and a studiously serious face, was an Austrian *Forstwirtschaftsmeister,* a master forester, an old-school profession which is still highly esteemed to this day, as it combines ecology and economics, the craftsmanship of precision logging and saw-milling with stewardship of natural timber resources. Schauberger spent an inordinate amount of time in the woods, often alone. His family motto was *Fidus in silvis silentibus* — Faithful to the quiet forests. He wrote: 'Even in earliest youth my fondest desire was to understand Nature and through such understanding to come closer to truth; a truth I was unable to discover either at school or in church. In this quest I was thus drawn time and time again into the forest.' And, invariably, towards the rivers and the trout which lived in them.

'I could sit for hours on end and watch the water flowing by without ever becoming tired or bored,' Schauberger wrote of his formative years in the forests of Bernerau in Steyerling. '. . . the fish, the mountain trout which lives in such rushing forest streams, reveals to us wonder upon wonder. How was it possible for this fish to stand so motionlessly, only steering itself with slight movements of its tail-fins, in this wildly torrential flow, which made my staff shake so much that I could hardly hang onto it? How was it able to flee upstream like a streak of greased lightning in mockery of all the laws of gravity? What forces enabled the trout, not only to overcome its own bodyweight so effortlessly and quickly, but also to overcome the weight of the water flowing against it?'

Unlike Norman Mclean, author of the classic *A River Runs Through It,* Schauberger came to be not haunted by waters, but inspired by them, and more than just aesthetically. From the moment he first watched trout hovering in a fast, muscular current, wondering about its fluid and effortless ways, his pragmatic Germanic mind began to focus on how to duplicate such phenomena and use them as a new form of technology. Thus the science of vortex mechanics was born, and with it a whole new way of looking at the movement of water, propulsion, even energy generation.

Daydreaming about Schauberger as I stalked up the Moeraki, I spooked another good fish, which held only two hand spans from the bank. It shot upstream like a blur and, in a domino effect, it knocked off of its perch another fish holding further up. Normally, I would curse my carelessness and lack of focus, but this time the grip of Schauberger's ideas was stronger than a short-lived tantrum. I never thought of it like this, but he was right. A spooked fish was not so much a lost chance as an opportunity to watch its mastery of water. 'I scared a large trout from its lair where it is able to feed and rest without effort,' Schauberger wrote of a similar experience. 'As if no law of gravity existed . . . the trout darted upstream . . . as if shot from a bow.'

So how did the trout manage their remarkable aquatic feats? After some more careful observations, Schauberger concluded it all had to do with the way trout breathed, the shape of their bodies and how they directed the flow of water over them. The trout, facing upstream, took in water through their mouths and expelled it through their gills. As this expelled water flowed over their streamlined bodies it began to spiral in the direction opposite to the current. Those vortices, like miniature water twisters, counteracted the power of the current to such a degree that the forces pulling the fish downstream and those holding it against the current were equalised. If the trout needed to accelerate upstream, Schauberger went on, it flapped its gills, breathing harder, creating a further vortex train down its flanks, increasing the upstream counter-thrust. The more rapid the gill movements, the faster the trout could moved upstream against the current.

This, of course, is a simplified explanation, without using vortex-dynamics jargon such as *non-euclidian paths of motion, cycloid space curve* and *hyperbolic centripetal spiral*. Looking up from the river, Schauberger realised that birds use the same principles of motion, that when air flows through and over their feathers during flight, strong counter-rotating vortices of updraught are formed, carrying and supporting their bodies.

He used to say that birds did not fly, they were flown, and fish did not swim, they were swum, by air and water respectively. Air and water in turn were a never-ending permutation of dynamic vortices — nature's preferred mode of movement. Nature abhorred straight lines, like the river canals made to a surveyor's ruler, said Schauberger, and everything in the universe, from galaxies and planetary systems through to the way plants grew and magnets and electricity worked, to how rivers flowed and water drained out of a bathtub — everything moved in three-dimensional spirals. Even

CDC dry

DNA, the blueprint for all life as we know it, is arranged in spirals, though Schauberger couldn't have known that in the 1930s.

All these notions remained the ramblings of a forest hermit until Schauberger began to implement what he had learnt from trout, birds and river flows into technologies of almost miraculous efficiency. His first project was a log flume for transporting timber out of a forest that was far from roads and rivers. He had it built as an elevated wooden chute, fifty kilometres long, but not straight as it ought to have been to a draughtsman's mind, but snaking and twisting its way down a valley like a mountain stream supported on trestles. His contemporary engineers guffawed with ridicule when Schauberger hit snags which inevitably accompany a pioneering venture, but he just sucked on his pipe and worked harder and smarter.

At every bend of his elevated river there were in-stream deflectors, which kept the rushing water spiralling on to itself and prevented the logs from bashing through the sides. The logs were heavy hardwood, and would not float even in a fast river, but down Schauberger's flume they went without a hitch, rotating in the centre of the pipe like bullets down a rifle barrel.

The flume was such a hit that experts from all over Europe came to view the design. By 1924, Viktor Schauberger was a consultant for log flumes and timber flotation for the Austrian state, with contracts in Bavaria and Yugoslavia. His treatise, entitled *Turbulence*, which described the braking function of vortices and their relation to water temperature, was accepted by the Austrian Academy of Science in January 1930.

By then, Schauberger had applied for numerous patents in water engineering and jet-turbine construction. One was for an apparatus to produce 'spring water', another for pipes that conducted this water so that it maintained its 'spring' quality. His propulsion system, again based on observations of trout, was originally called the 'trout turbine', but he later renamed it an 'implosion machine', after the idea that water imploded on itself as it spiralled down a natural vortex.

There are da Vinci-style drawings of his designs for a new type of submarine, one on which the Nazis, just coming to power, were particularly keen. The drawings show a remarkable trout-like shape. No, the machine wasn't designed to wag its rear end for propulsion, rather to use the same kind of current counter-thrust a trout produces to maintain its position against the flow of a river. Nature, Schauberger insisted, had had millions of years to perfect its designs. We could do no better than to observe and imitate.

Yet for all his insight, or perhaps because of them, throughout his life Schauberger remained a troubled genius. Despite the successes of his inventions, most of his concepts and the vast volume of his writings were just too esoteric to be taken seriously by his contemporaries who, in tune with Schauberger's affinity for vortices, considered him a rather loose screw. Imagine the patent office clerk, or an engineer hydrologist, reading this passage from Schauberger: 'A decade of observing the trout standing motionless in up-welling spring water has given me an insight into the deepest of Nature's secrets. Without any preconceptions, I simply let my gaze fall on the water as it flowed past. Only years later did I come to realise that running water attracts our consciousness like a magnet and draws a small part of it along in its wake.' But then, what else could you expect from a man who could get so easily entranced by the sight of flowing water.

Schauberger thus always remained at odds with the establishment and the academic world, and his fortunes swung like a wild pendulum, from derision to fame and back again. One moment he was an undesirable, strait-jacketed to a gurney in a mental institution in Mauer-Öhling, awaiting lethal injection; the next he was summoned to work for the Messerschmitt factory on engine cooling systems for the Heinkel jet. Like other visionaries, seemingly too far ahead of their time, he died a forlorn and disenchanted man in September 1958.

Today, Schauberger's ideas on vortex mechanics are enjoying

a vigorous revival. In Scandinavia, Germany and Russia there
are institutes dedicated to furthering his work. In the search
for cleaner, more efficient ways of propulsion and electricity
generation, it seems we may be ready to reconsider Schauberger's
trout turbine after all.

I could not catch a fish that day on the Moeraki River, my mind
too distracted with the bearded Austrian's ideas, troubled that
they did not find a wider audience or inspire a greater following.
I kept walking into trout and bungling my casts, and in the end
I just sat on the bank and watched the river flowing and whirling
upon itself, listening to its sibilation, which struck me as the
embodiment of silence, the whispered poetry of the vortices.

That night, in my river-mouth camp, as mosquitoes tried to
find weaknesses in my tent's netting and failed, I read more of
Schauberger. I had brought with me his book *Nature as Teacher* and a
part-biography, part-discussion of his ideas called *Living Water* by a
Swedish engineer, Olof Alexandersson.

The latter title and idea, clear as the trout streams from where it
came from, was both Schauberger's central message and the main
cause for his academic rejection. Water was neither a chemical nor
a resource, he insisted, but a living thing, the blood of the Earth,
which energised and renewed itself through vortical movement.
As such, it needed to be allowed to flow in its natural courses and
ways, twist and turn and cascade, free of obstructions like dams
and canals, shaded with riparian woods, which were critical for its
health. You can see how, in a climate of international rivalry for
industrial domination, when water was just the means of transport,
power generation and profits, such ideas would land Schauberger
in the cuckoo ward of a mental institution. In the end, he tired
of constantly battling against mainstream science and what he saw
as destructive and unsustainable technology. However, he offered
these words of warning: 'They call me deranged. The hope is that
they are right. It is of no greater or lesser import for another fool
to wander the earth. But if I am right and science is wrong — then
may the Lord God have mercy on mankind.'

It was Henry Spencer who introduced me to the work of
Schauberger, the same way he pointed me towards the writings
of Roderick Haig-Brown. The two men seemed to have a lot in
common: the ability to cast their free minds upon the flowing
rivers and to retrieve them later and draw unprecedented
conclusions. For Schauberger the rivers were the original *perpetuum
mobile*: for Haig-Brown they never slept. Haig-Brown wrote that
for him fishing was simply an excuse to be near rivers, and it seems

that Schauberger at least began to explain why moving water has such a mesmeric power upon us, how it can heal, energise and inspire profound thoughts and states of mind. For both men, just like they are for Henry Spencer and me, rivers were reverent entities, not just full of life, but alive themselves.

My thoughts drifted towards Henry. I had not heard from him for weeks. Had he found his own healing waters? Was he even still alive? The last time I had seen him he was even more reticent and withdrawn. His fishing clothes seemed a size too big for him, his face an odd mix of suntan and sickly greyness. He would only talk about fishing. The fishing was good, he said. It was excellent. Never better. But wouldn't it be, when you didn't know if there was another day ahead of you, if each fish you cast to might be the last one? If flowing water were so alive, as Schauberger insisted, couldn't it put some of that life back into Henry? Being with rivers most hours of every day, he surely made himself available for such a miracle. Without him, I thought, the world would be a poorer, less inspiring place. My world, for sure.

At my feet, Mops twitched, running in her sleep, woke herself up, groaned a sigh and stretched, then resumed the classic Airedale sleeping posture, one that resembles a squat knee-high chair fallen on its side, legs out straight and unbending. I, too, stretched and shook off the gloomy thoughts. I switched off my reading light and put the books away.

Outside, the frogs croaked and a morepork owl called against the soundscape of the river, which burbled and babbled as it entered the lake. Tomorrow, I promised myself, I'd be more focused on the fish; a hunter again, not a daydreaming bookworm. Still, I could not help but to bastardise Schauberger's family motto into something of my own, something I was sure he would approve. *Fidus in aquas, liquidus et libres.* Faithful to the rivers, flowing and free.

Just before I drifted into sleep I wondered if Schauberger fly-fished. I had no evidence one way or the other, but from his insights and the riverine moments of truth he gathered, I concluded he must have been one of us, a brother of the angle. Even if he did not carry a rod.

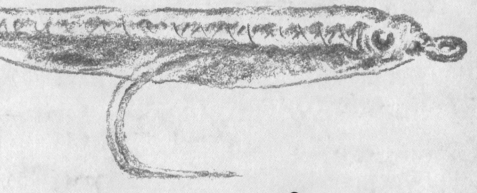

May

IT HAPPENED SO FAST AND SO SUDDENLY, the whole incident seemed unreal, even during the hours and days of shock and mourning that followed. One moment we were contemplating dinner, the next I was sprinting across the garden towards the open driveway gate, from behind which had just come feverish cries and swearing, cut off by the squeal of tyres, the thump of metal hitting flesh and an inhuman cry of pain.

My first thought was a prayer: *Please, don't let it be.* From the sounds I had heard I conjectured that one of my host's dogs must have been hit by a car in front of his eyes. This, I knew, he would take hard. The two endearing black mongrels were like his surrogate family.

In a way, my prayer was answered. Lying flat on the road, unmoving in a semicircle of onlookers, was neither one of his dogs. It was Mops, my inseparable companion of the past four years. She had followed my friend out as he went to close the gate, and another dog across the road had proved too great a temptation, at the worst possible time.

The speeding Subaru had run right over her chest, mashing the ribs and lungs. She was DOA as we rushed her to the vet. For a few moments she tried to eat the air, biting at it feebly, but then this, too, had stopped. Blood trickled from between her limp lips and from under her tail. Even the vet sobbed as she turned off the oxygen machine.

The following day I buried her on our favourite stretch of Wanaka beach, and turned around to face the void her departure had left; the sudden absence of that undemanding, eager-to-please and always happy canine presence, which until now had shadowed my every step. For a time I found myself gravitating towards people who still had dogs, an attempt to extend the continuity of my own dog experience. This was ultimately unsatisfying, because each bond between the human and the beast is as unique as its participants, and in such a relationship three's a crowd.

This time I could not even go to the rivers for solace because wherever I went Mops would always be there with me, and now she was not, and the emptiness was too much to bear. It was as if a part of me had gone missing, the fun part, the 'let's go and play' part, and gone with it was all the spontaneity and joy, even the joy of being with rivers — and that was frightening.

At times like this it is easy to feel singled out by fate, lost and alone in the misery of it all, incredulous that somehow, inexplicably, the world goes on as if nothing had happened, even if your private world had stopped, then shattered. Yet as friends and acquaintances wrote to me with words of comfort and empathy, or spoke them over the phone, there was not one person among them who had not experienced similar loss, whose consolations did not resonate with message: 'I know, I've been there.'

Even though I had not experienced it to such depths before, it was a revelation of sorts that profound loss is a natural human condition. The loss of a loved one — human or animal; it was not the number of legs that mattered but the depth of emotional engagement — was like birth, death and moments of deepest happiness. It affected everyone alive, even if the ways to deal with it were as many as there were people on the planet.

Somehow, in my grief, the words of Jack Kerouac came my way: 'Accept loss forever' — and I met them with rage and rebellion. Accept it? How could I? Mops had been with me 24/7, slept under my feet when I worked, and her infallible inner clock structured our days better than any PDA or diary. Breakfast. Work. Lunch. Walk. More work. Play chase in the garden. Afternoon siesta. Dinner. Evening walk. The perfection of a disciplined routine.

Accept the loss of all that? The days on rivers, the road trips, camping and campfire feasts, the forest walks, the purity of the friendship, the amicable silences and the communication that was almost telepathic? It seemed unthinkable, and yet, as the days went by, each numb and aimless, empty and cold, I began to realise old Jack was right. He knew this the way you know something not because someone tells you but because you have lived through it, and tried all other options, and none of them have worked, until you finally arrive at the conclusion we all have to reach in the end. There was no other way but to accept the loss, to stop clinging to what was, to let it go the way you watch a leaf floating downstream on the current and disappearing around the river bend. At least if you wanted to keep your sanity.

Still, it was easier said than done. Fortunately, through my gravitational pull towards 'dog people', I met Tony Turner later that month. Tony lives in Athol, near the bank of the Upper Mataura, and the passion he lives for is running sled dogs, namely a dozen huskies he hand-picked and brought home from Alaska.

The centrepiece of his home in Athol is a wooden cabinet with three rimu caskets, each containing the ashes of a dog. Vignette portraits of the three Malamutes adorn the caskets, and so do the dogs' names: Timitu, Ploddy and Badger. Among mushers, as sled-dog enthusiasts are called, this practice is not uncommon. Such is the bond between the human and the dog, forged through togetherness in overcoming dangers and hours of training and solitude, that long-distance mushers, surely among the hardiest souls on the planet, have been known to carry the ashes of their dogs the length of the world's most gruelling races, such as the Iditarod and the Yukon Quest. Just to take their favourite dogs for that one last run.

Fittingly, the rest of Tony's house is a veritable museum of mushing and all things sled dogs, decorated not so much with furniture but with pictures of dog races, old snow shoes, sleds and harnesses, all under the gaze of a larger-than-life portrait of a timber wolf. Tony's boyhood dream was to become a dog handler at Scott Base, in Antarctica, but he was born too late for that, so he did the next best thing: travelling to Alaska to learn the ropes of mushing.

His dogs are his life. 'They cost me a marriage, and they keep me poor,' he said with a never-mind-that smile, 'but they always give back more than you give them. By these standards, I have been a rich and fortunate man.

'When you see them streaking out in a line, feel the cold wind in your face and hear the sled runners planing on snow, you are at once a part of the pack, its leader and caretaker, and you know the pure unconditional happiness of doing what you were all born to do.'

In a world that insisted on going on regardless, even to the point of being mildly scornful after a time, as if to say 'get over it dude, it was *only* a dog', Tony Turner understood me better than most. He listened as I blubbered on about my adventures with Mops, but he did not commiserate. Instead, he offered the only plausible solution. Though I did not want to believe it at first, the only way to get over the loss of such a close companion was to mourn her with passion and then to get another dog. Their lives are shorter than ours, so a change of guard is inevitable.

Still, I could not fish or even go near a river for the ghosts of good times past were there to haunt me. Nevertheless, Tony's 'running with dogs' inspired me with an idea. I, too, began to run, not with dogs but with a dog, every day, sometimes for hours. A friend named Hope, true to her name, offered to 'loan' me a Border collie cross she had rescued from an abusive farmer. Keeping 'in behind', as if on an invisible tether, regardless of mileage or heat, Lynn made a perfect running companion.

The two refugees that we were, we ran the hills and forest plantations around Wanaka, six feet swallowing miles of trails, skin and fur getting covered with trail dust, washed by the rains, blow-dried by the nor'wester that came from the mountains. To begin with, I ran to forget and to numb the pain, hoping that some kind of absolution awaited at the end of all those miles, or at least a relief from the ill effects of the black hole that had opened and churned in my stomach.

At first, I found exhaustion, and with it the ability to sleep again, and this was already progress. Then, from the miles pounded out in solitude, came an odd sort of soothing strength, and slowly, over the weeks that followed, like an inner balm, this power stopped the void from spinning, and made it smaller, then smaller still, until all that remained was a scar. Lynn was just there, unquestioningly, as if running around the hill country like a banshee and getting absolutely wasted was the most natural thing to do.

In the end, though, Lynn and I were no match for each other, and I think she knew it, too. Airedales like Mops have an

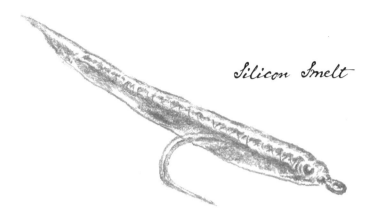

Silicon Smelt

exceptionally rich inner life, and show an almost eclectic curiosity. When you look into their chocolate-coloured eyes you know there is a lot going on behind them, even if most of it is pure mischief. By contrast, Lynn seemed bland and disinterested in most things, single-minded on shepherding, even though we did not have any sheep. She was a servant, while I sought a friend, and she hated water, and men with sticks, and this included fly rods.

Still, while she was with me, she travelled well, never complained or demanded anything, and was obedient to the point of obsession, always trying to please, anticipate even, as if to pre-empt the slightest possibility of human displeasure. All of which made what happened next an even bigger surprise.

I was having Sunday breakfast with a friend and, as always, had left Lynn in my camper, which she had come to consider a kind of luxury dog kennel on wheels. When I came back a couple of hours later, the inside of the camper was a scene of utter destruction. From my mobile library, Lynn selected a hard-to-find copy of Saint-Exupéry's *Vol de Nuit*, a borrowed biography of Beryl Markham and a Moleskine notebook half filled with my scribbles, and had ripped, shredded and scattered them all in small pieces around the camper's interior in an act of crazed and inexplicable rampage. She had pulled other stuff down from the overhead compartment where I kept my books, and was about to start on my down jacket. You could never raise your voice with her, or she would pee herself, and cower, and try to crawl into the tiniest corner, but this time I couldn't help it, which made the mess even worse.

I was still scolding her as we drove back home, but when we got into the house two messages awaited. One was from Hope. She had just placed a 'free to good home' ad in the local paper, and an excited family was coming all the way from Alexandra to meet Lynn and, all going well, to adopt her as a family pet. (This they would do: apparently, it was love at first sight, from every side.) The second message was from a dog breeder. That very morning, eleven Airedales had been born in Ashburton, and one of them was mine.

I looked at Lynn, trying to make herself invisible against her bed, and could not but wonder: how did she know?

Towards the end of May, with the news of the pups and all the good the running had done, I felt strong enough to go back to the rivers and the trout. The Southern Lakes and their tributaries always hold surprises, no matter how often you fish them. Maybe it's their sheer volume and depth that ensure we can never plumb all their secrets, or perhaps all angling discoveries have to be made one at a time, drip-feeding the lifetime of passion. I have lived and fished here for over a decade and a half but I can't say I really know fishing at the lakes. I do know some fragments of the lake experience: the early-spring nymphing, the bonanza of manuka beetles, the cicada time, when big browns patrol the surface of the deep-green water like something out of *Jaws*, and when a well-tied Yellow Humpy can yield two dozen fish before it starts to unravel. One thing I have learned about fishing the Southern Lakes is that whenever a new fragment appears, fitting it into the larger picture is going to be a treat. Without exceptions.

This time it was smelting. I used to go all the way to Taupo for a fix of shallow-water fishing to smelting trout, never thinking that such sport was possible on my home lakes. Sure, I've caught fish on smelt flies here, plying the rips of inflowing rivers during low-water winters, but in my ichthyological ignorance I assumed the voracious rainbows were taking the fly for a juvenile brown. Until Craig Smith enlightened me on the matter.

From March to May there is indeed a smelting season in the Southern Lakes, he said, and the fish, both brown and rainbows, are hunting not their own juveniles but land-locked whitebait. Just as the rivers are becoming tough to fish, with trout either paired up or extremely educated after a season of harassment, the smelting fish arrive, fresh from the lake. The rainbows especially, living deep and putting on excellent condition — Craig calls them 'footballs' — may have never seen an angler and an artificial fly. They are confident and aggressive, making for electrifying encounters. Furthermore, Craig said, he knew just the best places to fish for them.

Craig and I started guiding at about the same time, and, while I gave up guiding for the writing life, Craig continued, developing a solid clientele and impeccable reputation. Now, with the guiding season over, it was time for some R & D, which in the lingo of the pros translates into fishing for pleasure.

Thus, one perfectly still autumn morning, with the black sand of the beach in the shade of the mountain still frozen, we launched Craig's Stabicraft on to Lake Hawea, and he gunned the motor towards the mouth of the Hunter River. At the last minute, Craig had also invited Georgie Tolmay, and it was a masterful call. A Zimbabwean expat, Georgie grew up on the veldt, the daughter of an African safari guide, *stopped* game hunting at fourteen and learnt to fish on the Zambezi tigerfish. Her manners, voice and accent were so unmistakable that when I closed my eyes I could imagine her reading the opening lines of *Out of Africa*: 'I had a farm in Africa at the foot of the Ngong Hills . . .'

Fluffing up my down jacket against the wind chill, I asked her what it is about fly-fishing that motivates her to wade into icy rivers at dawn. 'When I'm fishing I don't think of anything else,' she replied. 'No business, no responsibilities. My mind and soul are clear and carefree. This is time for me to just be me. And there is so much to learn, it's a total thrill.' With this particular kind of smelting there would indeed be much to learn.

Smelting is not the correct term for what we were about to do, though it's descriptive of the technique, if not of the species. There are no smelt in the Southern Lakes; all efforts to introduce them have failed. What we take for smelt is in fact whitebait, a mix of galaxiid species, almost the same as the whitebait which stream in every spring from the ocean and cause an entire tribe of people to abandon whatever they are doing and try to net the little squirts.

Like their ocean-going kin, lake whitebait also migrate upstream to spawn, and, likewise, they only make it into the estuaries, where they deposit their eggs. The resulting juveniles are washed downstream to complete the whitebait life cycle. Trout follow the adult whitebait, eager for one last big feast before their own spawning runs, and they slash through the sandy shallows, hitting the translucent fingerlings with a ferocity usually reserved for cicadas. It is a sight that shifts the angler's heartbeat into double-time. At least until he or she starts casting.

There is a definite knack to sight-fishing with a smelt fly, a necessary sensitivity of touch and timing, and getting it just right can be a trying experience. I'm not bragging if I say I can put a fly where I want it to be within a cast or two, and I know about line drag and the other nuances of presenting a fly. Hell, I used to teach it! So when my turn came to fish on this frosty morning I was confident. We sighted a good brown zigzagging its way along the shallow silt shelf. I cast square across the river, plonking the smelt a good two metres up and above, sending it on an inevitable collision course with the trout.

Easy. The fish saw the fly, and turned and attacked with a burst of speed. A positive take if I ever saw one. I gave it the required 0.4786 second delay, then lifted the rod, ready to yahoo.

Nothing. Just a pile of slack line coiling on itself like a broken rubber cord.

The fish returned to its beat, unperturbed, while I untangled. Bad luck? Well, not if it happens four times in a row, on the same trout. Especially if, in identical circumstances, Craig hooked his two fish cleanly during their first attack. It was clearly a matter of skill. There was finesse and fine tuning required before those volts and amperes could travel up the fly line, into the rod handle and the hand, and on to fire the entire nervous system and make the heart speed up and glow.

On another fish Craig demonstrated his technique again. Cast well up and beyond the fish, mend upstream and hold the rod tip down to let the fly sink before it starts to swing. Then, as the fly approaches the fish, give the line a gentle tug. Raising the rod a few inches and pulling in the slack is just enough. Watch the fish chase and take. Then, ah, the secret, a *test strip*, because in their gluttonous rush the trout can often miss the fly, just as the inevitable drag whisks it away from in front of their snouts.

In my own vocabulary, a test strip is something photographic labs used to produce in pre-digital days, though I guess the term could also refer to a job interview at certain types of night club. For Craig, it meant a subtle tightening of the fly line to feel if the fish actually took the fly. If it didn't, the manoeuvre animated the smelt, adding urgency to its movement and a brutal take would often follow almost instantly.

There are some nineteen known species of galaxiid in New Zealand — among them the giant kokopu, koaro, long jawed and flathead galaxias, banded kokopu and dwarf inanga — but mercifully they can be all imitated with just one fly, the elegantly simple Silicon Smelt. Even on a long leader the Silicon Smelt casts like a dream, and you can present it as accurately as you would a dry. But the Smelt has one inherent problem you need to keep in mind. Especially on long casts, the soft tapered tail has a tendency to catch on the hook and stay at right angles to it. As you cast and

'When I'm fishing I don't think of anything else . . .
My mind and soul are clear and carefree. This is time
for me to just be me. And there is so much to learn, it's
a total thrill.' Georgie Tolmay
    . . . and she gets the results, too.

Fishing for smelting trout is an exciting game of pursuing fast and aggressive fish (top). Georgie lays out a long cast across the unforgiving still water of a lagoon braid (bottom).

Sight-fishing in edge-of-the-lake still water is perhaps the greatest secret of fly-fishing in New Zealand. Lake Wanaka, just one of many locations, is as hard as it gets and just as satisfying.

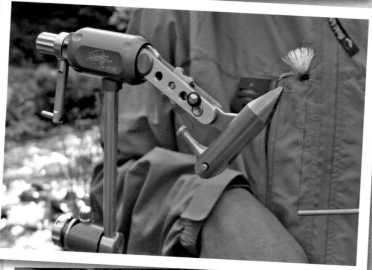

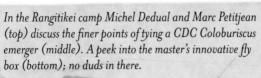

In the Rangitikei camp Michel Dedual and Marc Petitjean
(top) discuss the finer points of tying a CDC Coloburiscus
emerger (middle). A peek into the master's innovative fly
box (bottom); no duds in there.

Ever wondered how the damselflies do it (top)? On Lake Otamangakau, Marc Petitjean lays a perfect aerial cast to uncommonly reluctant fish (middle), while Anaru (bottom) goes for a more pragmatic off-the-water approach, Tongariro-style.

'No man seeking a full life should have to face his fate without a dog.' Jim Thornton. In memory of Mops, the best dog that ever was, and to Maya, who is even better.

I have never caught a fish on such a 'crippled' smelt, and it pays to check the fly every few casts. With a bit of experience you can actually hear if it has gone crooked as you cast it. The sound is a light fluttering, not unlike when a dry fly picks up a tiny leaf.

retrieve it, the cock-eyed assemblage becomes a veritable propeller, putting a fast-accumulating spin on the leader and making a real mess if you continue unaware.

I have never caught a fish on such a 'crippled' smelt, and it pays to check the fly every few casts. With a bit of experience you can actually hear if it has gone crooked as you cast it. The sound is a light fluttering, not unlike when a dry fly picks up a tiny leaf.

Not all smelt flies are made equal, either. The cheap, round squirts may be okay for the broken water at a rip, but for fishing to a sighted trout you want unrefusable quality. Such smelts have flattened tails which, Craig insists, ensure an all-important trout-triggering flutter when they move across the current.

As the day unfolded we stalked the braids of the Hunter, the estuarine oxbows and channels that the river has cut into a valley floor that is as flat as a football field. We hooked more fish, and lost some, too, because the hooks of the Silicon Smelt are large and don't always set well. This we did not mind. Being connected to a charging fish even for a few moments was electrifying enough.

The fish were good, each averaging around 5 lbs in weight, and about as much in horsepower. There was only one thing which was ruining an otherwise perfect day: it was already late afternoon, and Georgie still did not have a fish.

Her casting was letting her down, especially when a trout was in sight and the adrenalin surged. Speed of delivery is crucial with these trout. They are fast cruisers, and you often have to run and cast to keep putting the fly in front of their noses. Craig offered hints here and there, and Georgie's casting was becoming more accurate, but the improvement came too late. The sun disappeared behind the mountains, and with polaroiding gone and the temperatures plummeting, we had to beat a quick retreat to the boat and the open water.

Minutes later, we were back in the sun, with the warmth and light streaming in through a deep V-shaped gap in the mountains, aligned like a gun sight with the mouth of the Dingle Burn. We parked the boat and ran towards the braided rip, wanting to make the most of the waning day. And a good thing we did.

With two consecutive casts, and with the current straightening the line and helping her to feel the takes, Georgie hooked two fat rainbows that proved to be the largest fish of the day: silver torpedoes smudged with crimson. Since she was using a light #5 rod, Georgie screamed and cursed in elegant Italian as her forearms cramped and turned into jelly against the sheer pulling power of such magnificent fish.

An hour later, we were at Craig's place overlooking Lake Hawea, watching the expanse of water being swallowed by the dusk. The log fire roared quietly and we sipped Glenfiddich, to dispel the last of the chill and celebrate a perfect day.

In the retrospective mood such moments bring about, I casually mentioned how amazing our lakes were, how, just when you thought you knew a place, it would always surprise you, and how good it was trying to learn a place but never knowing it all.

'Well, actually, there is another thing you may want to try, which not even many locals know about . . .' Craig grinned from behind his glass.

What was it? Another one of his secrets? I asked, but he would not say.

'Oh, go on. Do tell,' Georgie insisted.

'Well, there are those spring creeks on the Coast, and in the spring . . .' he began, and smiled again.

Georgie and I were all ears.

June

 IN THE CALENDAR OF NEW ZEALAND
fly-fishing, I've always found June to be the most
awkward month. Down south, the days are cold and
short. Most of the waters are closed, the insect life is in
deep hibernation and the brown trout are spawning, having lost
all interest in everything else. The rainbows are about, in good
condition, more aggressive than ever, and imminently catchable if
you can brave the depressing weather and the inversion layer. The
thick, grey, heavy and often drizzly cloud is caused by the seasons
turning from autumn to winter and it seems to sap all joy and
colour out of the landscape and the people, bringing about the
symptoms of sunshine deprivation. In Scandinavia, where they get
a lot more of it, people call this suicide weather. For many years
now, my seasonal cure for this malaise has been to head north for
the sunny expanse of Lake Taupo and its tributaries.

In this country of trout, no place is steeped in more tradition
and angling lore than Taupo. On rivers like the Tongariro,

Tauranga–Taupo and Waitahanui, every pool has a name and a history, and these days often half a dozen anglers.

In 1883, the Auckland Acclimatisation Society hatched and reared the country's first batch of rainbow trout, which most likely came from Sonoma Creek, near San Francisco, where they are known as steelheads (sea-run rainbows) and grow up to 15 kg. On the morning of 24 February 1898, one Forrestina Ross of Wellington released a pannikin of the first rainbows into a tributary of the Tongariro River. More liberations soon followed, and within four years the Waikato rainbows were weighing in at 3.5–4 kg, and in Taupo a 10-kg fish was caught five years after the first release. In one season, 56,000 fish, totalling 112 tonnes, were taken from the lake and its rivers. Trout were so plentiful they were given to local farmers as pig fodder.

Then, in 1912, the size and the quality of Taupo trout rapidly deteriorated. As an introduced predator, they had caused a collapse of the native koaro population, their main food source in the lake. To remedy the situation, gamekeepers embarked on a massive trout-netting exercise, a solution that worked for a while and took the Taupo fishery through a short-lived golden era in the mid-1920s.

But within a few years there were again too many trout and not enough food. This time the wardens employed a different strategy: rather then culling the trout they increased their food. Common smelt, a translucent, whitebait-like fish, first introduced in the Rotorua lakes in 1907, was brought to Lake Taupo. It spread like a locust and has thrived there ever since in a state of continuous overabundance. The trout population bounced back with vigour.

Those early years were also a time of great secrecy. One of the Taupo angling sagas tells of an Irishman named Ernest de Lautour, a former curator of South African hatcheries, who was involved with, and subsequently blamed for, the failed introduction of cisco herring, an experimental trout fodder preceding smelt. Following this miscarriage, de Lautour had vanished.

George Mannering, better known for his early attempts to climb Mt Cook but also a fine and passionate angler, recounted de Lautour pulling in some big rainbows out of a then-unknown river: 'I discovered he was wet fly-fishing for rainbows, which none knew were there except him . . . He used to tie his own flies on the bank — never kept spare ones lest others should find them. He just had a bunch of feathers in one pocket, and some coloured string and hooks in another. He had his camp on a Maori burial ground

> *Grey arrived with his entourage and fished for marlin in the Bay of Islands and for trout in Taupo . . . 'If Zane went out with a mosquito net to catch minnows, he could make it sound like a Roman Gladiator setting forth to slay whales in the Tiber . . .'*

to keep his things safe, as this was "tapu". . . He kept this river to himself all the season.'

The river was the Waitahanui, and de Lautour had his camp — a reed hut and a tiny garden for which he paid rent of two bags of flour a year — near its best pools. He lived there on fish and his vegetables for seven years, until the idyll came to an abrupt end when he poisoned a litter of his landlord's pigs, which kept rooting up his garden.

He was banished from Waitahanui, but by then the secret was already out, and someone else was about to trumpet it to the world. His name was Zane Grey, and though skilled with a rod and reel, he was even better with his pen. In the US, Grey made a considerable fortune by writing cowboy romances, and such was the power of his literary élan that in 1926 the New Zealand government invited him to fish here in the hope that his words would promote the fledgling trout and big-game fishing tourism industry.

Grey arrived with his entourage and fished for marlin in the Bay of Islands and for trout in Taupo. And although, as one of his biographers, Robert Davis, wrote, 'If Zane went out with a mosquito net to catch minnows, he could make it sound like a Roman Gladiator setting forth to slay whales in the Tiber', it seemed that Grey's antipodean adventures needed no literary embellishment. The resulting book, *Tales of the Angler's Eldorado, New Zealand* — became an instant classic, and gave New Zealand an angling reputation that has not faded since.

But back then Grey's enthusiasm went further than it was welcomed. He was so thrilled by the quality of fishing in

Taupo that he wanted to buy the entire Tongariro River. The negotiations were apparently advanced, but fortunately for us modern anglers, in 1926 the government passed a law which guaranteed free access to all rivers in the Taupo area.

Grey's dream of exclusively owning what has been consistently considered one of the best trout rivers in the world did not eventuate. Disappointed, he bought a cabin on the Rogue River in Oregon, where he wrote and fished for steelheads, and which, through his prose, became a shrine of the American West. On his front porch, Grey installed a swivel fighting chair that he rigged up with a system of pulleys and weights, like a gym machine but with a fishing rod instead of a bench press. There he worked out, preparing for his fishing expeditions. In this chair, as the world readied for the outbreak of World War II, he died of heart failure at the age of sixty-eight, pumping iron the angler's way.

I have a soft spot for Taupo, and especially the Turangi area, for it was here I had the formative experiences which shaped me as a fly-fisherman.

On my first foray there, in a Turangi hostel, I met Paul Arden, an Englishman whose lobster-tan face bore the unmistakable bug-eye imprint of a pair of polarising sunglasses. Back home, he worked as a casting tutor and representative for a fishing gear manufacturer, but every English off season he came to New Zealand for his share of the angler's Arcadia. Where else but here, he asked me, could you fish for world-class trout every day of the year for a mere $95?

'All rivers in the UK are privately owned, so fishing is exclusive and expensive,' he told me as we motored in his aluminium dinghy towards the Tongariro delta. 'You pay the owner and get an allocated stretch of the river, say 200 yards of the left bank, from one fence to another. For a well-known chalk stream like the Test or the Itchen it can cost you a hundred quid a day, and you have to book months ahead. And these are the rivers where you *can* go. There are many more where you can't, not unless you have a "Sir" to your name.'

We beached the boat on a gravel bar and waded up one of the delta channels, thigh-deep in the water, volcanic sand squirting between our toes with every step. That day we surprised many fish. One which remains fixed indelibly in my memory lay mid-stream, a big brown trout finning just enough to maintain its

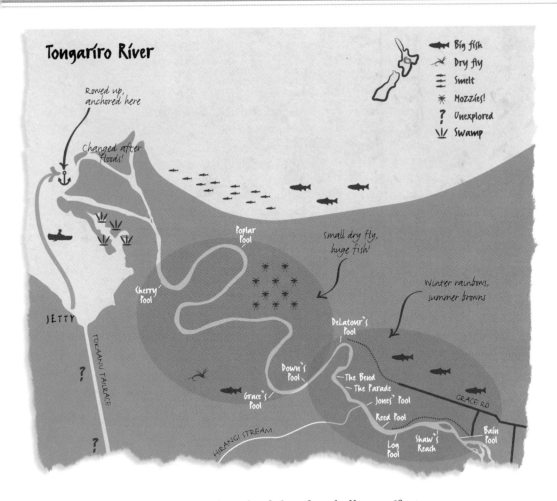

Tongariro River

Rowed up, anchored here

Changed after floods!

JETTY

Cherry Pool

Poplar Pool

Small dry fly, huge fish!

Down's Pool

Grace's Pool

Grace RD

DeLatour's Pool

Winter rainbows, summer browns

— The Bend
— The Parade

Jones' Pool

Reed Pool

Log Pool

Shaw's Reach

Bain Pool

HIRANGI STREAM

TOKAANU TAILRACE

Big fish
Dry fly
Smelt
Mozzies!
Unexplored
Swamp

position. I cast repeatedly, but the fish refused all my offerings, sometimes ignoring them completely, sometimes coming in for a closer look, then turning back without a take.

My hands shook every time I changed a fly.

'Here, try this,' Paul whispered over my shoulder. From his backpack, he produced a wooden box the size of a laptop computer, which, like a portable entomological museum, contained sheets and sheets of insects, all of them artificial.

Earlier that day Paul had told me that, as a boy, he had owned a set of aquaria in which he kept not fish but bugs. He watched them grow and metamorphose, from eggs to larvae to nymphs to adults. He studied their behaviour and habits, then tied precisely matching imitations. Now he carried the fruit of this and other research in his wooden box: 8000 different flies in all colours and sizes — at shop prices worth about $20,000 — covering most foreseeable fishing scenarios.

He handed me a large dry fly, which I tied on and cast. For a few moments it floated on the surface like a bird's feather before the trout snatched it the way a dog snatches a stick. That speckled fish was a glory to hold and behold.

We caught and missed other fish that day before dusk fell, followed by the warm summer night. Stumbling in the darkness, we waded downstream, sweeping the way ahead for obstacles with our rods until the dagger of a young moon came out to guide us.

At first, the outboard would not start, and then it did, but the boat's lights short-circuited. We puttered at a snail's pace, groping our way through the narrow channel from one marker to another, alone on the lake, laughing a lot. We seemed to step outside of time and into our boyhood again, playing Huck Finn and Tom Sawyer adrift in a clapped-out boat. I thought there was no other place I would rather be, and I knew that, from that day on, fly-fishing was something I'd do for as long as I could walk and hold a rod.

This was years before Paul Arden started his immensely successful website, www.sexyloops.com, before he became 'the world's most expensive fly casting instructor'. I did have some casting tuition with him that time, gasping at the seeming impossibility of having the entire fly line out in the air and not collapsing, or watching the sniper-like precision of his bow-and-arrow casts from the junglified banks of the lower Tongariro. But my major breakthrough, a fly-casting 'Aha!' moment, did not come until I had a practice session with Carol Harwood, also in Turangi.

Nowadays, after years of having a callus from a fly rod, just under the ring finger where a wedding band would touch it, I no longer think of the mechanics of casting, and concentrate on the fish instead, the way you watch the road and not the gear stick while driving. But back then, I was obsessed with the correct form, frustrated with the impossibility of understanding such seemingly simple yet hellishly complex movements. The soaring arc of the line is like an angler's aerial signature — an illegible scribble in the case of a beginner, calligraphy in motion when performed by an expert.

I know better now. As with calligraphy, you can't really understand casting, and even if you did this would not necessarily make you a better caster. The secret to casting is that you have to *feel it* — feel the loading of the rod, feel how much line you have in the air, feel it so that you can do it with your eyes closed. It was Carol Harwood who showed me that.

When I met her, she was a sprightly woman in her sixties, still nursing a sprained elbow from tussling with a 10-kg salmon in Alaska. She learned to fish the hard way, she told me, by watching and emulating her husband, Frank, a Yorkshire-born Turangi guide.

He was a merciless teacher. He made her tie flies, or rather one fly, and until it was absolutely perfect he would shave it off the hook shank with a razor blade and make her start again.

Thanks to her aptitude with needlework, Carol gave him few opportunities to wield the blade, but still, for the first year of her tough apprenticeship she just stood behind Frank in the river, looking over his shoulder and listening.

That was many years ago. When we met, this 'five-foot-nothing old girl', as she described herself, had just been admitted to the ranks of the New Zealand Professional Fishing Guides Association, one of only two female guides in the country at the time.

On her Turangi lawn, Carol took me through one of Frank's diabolical exercises. The daisies were out in force, and she pointed out a clump of three about ten metres away. With a quick backcast she had the line in the air. She paused momentarily to let it straighten behind her back, then her forearm came down like a hammer, her thumb on the rod's cork handle, sighting one of the flowers. The line shot forward like a whip, its tip patted the daisy's head and left it quivering. One! A backcast, another daisy. Two! Another backcast and a miss, though not by much.

'Oops! I'll do it again,' she said, her face focused as if she were threading a needle. One! Two! Three! The daisies quivered.

'Your turn,' she said, handing me the rod. 'Pick your flowers.'

I made a couple of false casts to judge the distance, then let the line fly and — lo and behold — the line-tip hit a daisy on the head!

'Excellent!' Carol applauded, 'See, it's not that hard!'

I smiled uneasily. The daisy I had aimed for was another metre to the side.

That June, walking Michel Dedual's dog along the Tongariro River, I saw Henry Spencer again. We were crossing a wooden bridge, and Henry was fishing the pool immediately below. He looked stooped and frail, but his casting was as beautiful as ever. With great deliberateness he made each cast into a masterly brushstroke. He was nymphing, using the ungainly Tongariro trio: an epoxy bomb, an egg and an orange indicator that always reminds me of the pompom on some brands of ski hats.

Most people struggle with such a rig. I, for one, have always considered it too crude and awkward. The epoxy bomb ruins all the aesthetics of casting and makes you want to wear a crash helmet to protect yourself from your own casts.

Yet watching Henry, you'd think he was casting a small dry fly. He let the line drift all the way down, and paused for the current to straighten it completely. Then, with a smooth and effortless flick he lifted the line off the water and, without any false casting at all, placed it upstream where he wanted it to go. There was the sound of a kiss as the line peeled off the water, the swoosh of the pompom through the air and the plop of the bomb as the line settled upstream.

It looked easy, but looks are deceptive. Henry was so focused on what he was doing — the cast, the indicator bobbing in the current, twitching as the bomb bounced off the bottom rocks — that he was oblivious to everything around him. Leaning against the guardrail of the bridge, I watched him for a long time, but he never once looked up, and I did not dare to call or to go down to him and break the spell. Instead, I retreated along the creaking planking, tiptoeing back as if I had just walked into someone's intimate moment. It was likely I was seeing him for the last time. If anything, I thought, this was how I'd want to remember him, doing what he loved, and doing it so well.

July

 A COUPLE IN THEIR LATE SIXTIES WHOM
I visit regularly on my fishing forays into Southland
have a peculiar trout ritual which they observe
annually with the zeal of votaries. They have both fished for
most of their lives, probably clocking a century between them
if they cared to add up the years, though these days streamside
mobility has become an issue. Still, every year in June or July,
depending on the timetable of nature itself, they await a much
anticipated phone call from a like-minded couple up-country
whose farm borders the Mataura River where it comes out the
Nokomai Gorge.

The day of the call would always be short and cold but sunny,
and they would stoke up their coal range before they left.
Most likely, Nancy would have baked scones the night before,
maybe sweet shortbread as well, and she would pack it all into
Tupperware containers with jars of butter and jam, and fill up
a big wide-mouthed Thermos with tea. They would leave their

valley which in winter is often foggy and head up the Mataura,
towards the sunshine and the site of their pilgrimage.

They would collect their friends on the way through and drive
to where the river is wide and shallow, its bottom cobbled with
gravel of just the right size. Then, on a high bank with a grand view
of it all, they would spread out their chequered blanket, the food
and the tea cups, and have their lunch in amiable silence, watching
the trout spawning in the river below.

'There'd be hundreds of fish in this particular spot,' Nancy
said, 'all brown trout, but black now in their spawning colours.'
Many fish would be paired up, hovering in fast-flowing water
over lighter patches on the bottom which marked the redds they
had dug up with their own bodies. And there would always be the
freelancers and the opportunists, the under-aged and the Johnny-
come-latelies, who would try to add a squirt of their own genes
when the action over a redd had reached its decisive moment.

The two couples would sit and feast on the food they'd brought
and the scene before them, and when the low winter sun moved
over far enough to begin to glare off the water, making it dazzling
and opaque, they would pack up and leave, reassured by the
plenitude of fish and the knowledge that, in their world, all was
well for the year to come. No matter what news of doom and gloom
the little electronic 'window on the world' brought into their living
rooms every night, these four knew there was also a larger window
into a larger world, a liquid window into an entire universe of lithe
beauty and mesmerising grace, and even a once-a-year glimpse
into it was a potent antidote against the ills of civilisation. The
trout were spawning, as numerous as ever, and with the coming
new season and warmer weather, they and their offspring would
soon be rising to dries and picking nymphs off the bottom, their
sleek golden bodies tilting sideways as they did so. Then, even
if you didn't have a rod with you, the very sight of them would
gladden your heart.

'Don't really need to fish for them,' Nancy said matter-of-
factly, brushing off any further enquiries into what she simply
called a lunch by the river. 'It's just good to know they are there,
and they're doing well.'

I know of no other fish, apart from salmon, that elicit such
affectionate attention. But I know that Nancy, her husband Rollie
and their friends are not alone in their sentiments. My own
invitation to witness the wonder of spawning trout came from
Michel Dedual, my ichthyologist friend from Turangi. Across
from the Rangipo Prison and up the Whitikau Stream, a tributary

of the Tongariro, we crept along the stony bank, crawling the last couple of metres to the water's edge. There, in water so shallow their backs were half above the surface, I saw several hundred rainbow trout jostling for redd real estate and spawning partners. It was Darwinian dynamics at their most fundamental.

The trout, preoccupied with the business of sex, were so close we could reach out and touch them. Michel has been in Turangi long enough to acquire a Billy T. James giggle and knows trout intimately. He has caught and eaten them, radio-tracked and dived with them, and watched them for hours, yet even he could not contain his excitement at the sight of such embarrassing abundance.

'Amazing, huh?' he nodded at the milling hundreds of trout. 'As a fisheries scientist I follow closely what happens with fish populations around the world — in Alaska, Patagonia and Europe. They all pale next to this. There is no better place for wild rainbow trout than the Central North Island. New Zealanders — even the locals here in Taupo and Turangi — just don't realise how good we have it.'

Taupo's brown trout spawn earlier than the rainbows, Michel explained. They move up the rivers in April and May, and the resident rainbows often gather just below their redds, feeding on eggs that are washed downstream. But the rivers that drain the Volcanic Plateau contain large amounts of pumice and small stones, some of which are similar in shape and size to trout eggs. 'I've caught rainbows with their bellies full of ova-size pumice,' Michel said. 'They feel as crunchy as bean bags.'

Why is Taupo such an outstanding fishery?

Michel explained that it was a combination of things. The water is very clean, because there is relatively little farming around the lake edges. There are buffer zones of forest along the length of the inflowing rivers and streams, and their bottoms are made of porous, volcanic gravel, which purifies the water like a carbon filter. Then there is the profusion of smelt in the lake, which the trout can hunt with little effort. Also, the fish can spawn all year round. Although they prefer the colder months, spawning runs happen in summer as well. But, most importantly, the entire system is large, diverse and robust. If a cataclysm should strike at one end — a flood, localised pollution, or even a volcanic eruption, as happened a few years ago — there will be rivers and streams at the other end which are not affected.

The net result is that the trout population is healthy and self-sustaining. Michel and his fellow fisheries scientists monitor it closely because in Taupo, where 60,000–70,000 fishing licences are sold annually, angling is big business, bringing close to $100 million a year to the local economy. Using echo-sounding surveys, scientists can estimate the number of fish of legal angling size in the lake. It fluctuates between 150,000 and 200,000.

The last couple of years, however, the fish have been even more numerous, but smaller. The minimum legal size has been lowered from 45–40 cm and fisheries managers went as far as encouraging anglers to keep the legal-size fish they caught, rather than putting them back. This brought about a re-examination of the logic and the finer points of the practice of catch-and-release.

Catch-and-release is a concept impossible to explain, let alone justify, to someone who has not arrived at it as part of their trout-fishing journey. In the beginning, you just want to catch a fish, then many fish — the more the better. Then you move on to sight-fishing, and start targeting bigger trout or favouring a particular style, say a dry fly, over any other. By then, you've become skilled and proficient, accumulated a critical mass of experience. When you spot a fish, you often have a fair chance of catching it — 50:50 perhaps, sometimes better. Gone are the frustrations, and most of the tangles, and an occasional goof-up is a reason to laugh, not to curse.

It is at this point, at least according to the traditional progression, that you start catching too many fish. Or perhaps from the outset you've subscribed to Lee Wulff's ideal that trout are too precious to be caught just once. So you release the fish you catch, often all of them, and if anyone starts telling you that you shouldn't, your own hackles of temper and indignation rise to rival Lee's best Royal Wulffs. If you've travelled this far down the glorious road of trout fishing, walk with me a few more steps, so that you can be confident that the fish you release have the best possible chance of survival.

Picture two men in a boat anchored in a perfect spot on the drop-off at one of Taupo's river mouths. The lake is glassy and the delightful kauri boat is named *Nefer-TT*, after the Tauranga–Taupo River, the TT to those in the know. The fishing is good, really good, and every few minutes the tip of one of the rods quivers. The owner of the rod strikes excitedly, but then, more often than not, his face drops slack with disappointment. He is still stripping the line but the shooting head is running free again, the tip of the rod no longer quivering and bending. Every time this happens, the older of the two men, only slightly older, picks up his notebook and scribbles something into a window of a neatly drawn table.

As I said, the fishing is good, or at least it would be if we were putting our best tackle forward. By now, I've had seven or eight solid, hang-on-to-your-rod kind of strikes, but landed only one fish. My illustrious companion Michel Dedual is doing better, though not much better considering that this is his home river, and in any case, it's rare to see him lose a fish.

The problem is, we are testing circle hooks as a part of a research project to which Michel is contributing data. Circle hooks are, well, circular, unlike the prevalent half-ovals, and they are said to be kinder on the fish. True enough, so far they have been. Using them, we've barely managed to hook a trout.

The advantage of circle hooks is supposed to be the fact they are easy to remove. Here, too, I cannot argue. They are so easy to remove the trout can do it without any assistance from the angler, and often even despite all efforts to the contrary. In the name of science, however, we persevere — though ultimately the idea of introducing and promoting circle hooks to the wider angling community will be abandoned. The consensus is that the action of setting such hooks is so different from that of standard hooks that the angler's muscle memory, formed and honed on so many fish, is too ingrained to be unlearned and re-programmed.

So what does all this have to do with catch-and-release? Well, a lot, because our TT experiment was a part of the same quest: how to make the fishing experience if not less traumatic then at least more tolerable to the fish we so adore, dream about, idolise and worship.

Of course, not everyone considers trout an embodiment of poetry in aquatic motion, and looking around on the river it is possible to conclude that trout idolisers are the minority. The greater Taupo area, for one, is considered a 'keep' fishery, meaning anglers keep all they legally can, and put back only what's slabby or under size. On the rivers and lakes here you see some dreadful mistreatment of trout: fish kept 'fresh' and alive in inch-deep puddles of water, fish booted up the rocky bank, only to be roughly shaken off the hook and booted back into the river. Too small, you see.

For the greater part of his professional life as a trout scientist in Turangi, Michel has been crusading for the welfare of the fish and for better education of anglers, whether they fish for the table or for sport.

'There should be no difference in the treatment of the fish until the moment you decide to either keep it or put it back,' he says. 'Playing a fish until it's exhausted beyond recovery is detrimental to both the taste and its survival if released. So, the number-one rule is to use the heaviest tippet that will do the job and reel the fish in as quickly as possible.'

I'd add this: if you really love trout and care about their well-being after release, use barbless hooks whenever you can, especially with large-size hooks, 12s and below. You may end up with a few 'long-range' releases, but weren't you going to put the fish back anyway? Often, though not always, after the electrifying moment of the take and hook-up, the playing and landing of the fish is almost routine. Yet this is the part which stresses the fish most, at least until you get it into the net.

The next phase is even more important. With the right kind of net you can significantly improve the fish's odds of surviving its encounter with you. Soft-mesh nets are now becoming *de rigueur*, at least among conscientious guides and anglers who fish a lot and catch plenty of fish. The older nets — the woven-knotted type — are harsh enough to abrade the trout's skin and scrape off some of its protective mucus. If you don't think so, ask yourself why you have to rinse these nets after every fish and why they stiffen up when dry.

Now that you have a barblessly hooked fish in a soft-mesh net, what next?

'Wet your hands,' Michel says. 'This is really basic, but you'd be surprised how many anglers forget to do it in the moment of excitement. Then, above all else, keep the fish in the water, and if possible do not touch it at all.'

Why can touching the fish be so harmful to them?

'Remember, they are cold-blooded,' he says. 'Being touched with warm hands — and even on a cold day your hands are likely to be twenty degrees warmer than the trout's body temperature — is something they never experience under water. It gives them both a shock and a fright. We've done studies on stress in hooked fish, measuring the level of cortisol, which you could call the stress hormone. The levels go sharply up during the hook-up and the fight, but they absolutely sky-rocket the moment you touch the fish with your warm hands.' With an infra-red camera, you can see the human fingerprints on the fish's skin for hours, sometimes days after the experience. They look unmistakably like burn marks.

Helping the fish continue breathing is even more critical. Imagine you've been outsmarted by a powerful predator, run

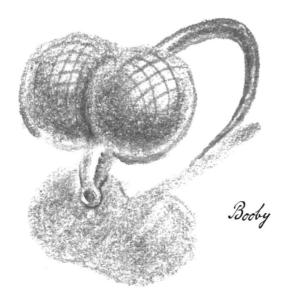

Booby

down and cornered by it. You've done your best to escape, you've sprinted hard and fast for as long as you could, but now you are exhausted and spent, gasping and wheezing for air, yet still barely getting enough of it. At this moment your captor grabs you and puts your head under water.

'This is how a fish must *feel* when you lift it *out* of the water,' Michel goes on. 'Without water running over its gills, the fish cannot breathe, so while you're weighing it, showing it off to your mates and taking endless pictures, the fish is gagging for oxygen. Of course, it doesn't make any sound, so you don't know. If the fish could scream, you'd never take it out of the water.'

So keep the net with the fish in the water, he counsels. Remove the hook with pliers or a similar tool, then, if the trout is free of tangles, simply upend the net and let it go.

This would be the ideal scenario, but what if the fish is hooked badly or deep, as often happens with egg imitations and Boobies? 'The fish would be better off if you just cut the tippet and left the fly where it is,' Michel says. 'The surgery you perform trying to extract the hook is likely to do more damage than the hook itself. Like all wild creatures, fish have amazing healing abilities, and they'll eventually work the hook out. This is preferable to squeezing the fish between your knees, forcing its jaws open and sticking a pair of pliers down its throat. Even though you may see it swimming away, the fish is unlikely to survive such an ordeal.'

If you need to hold a fish — say to revive it after the fight — grasp it firmly by the tail peduncle (where the body is narrowest at the base of the tail fin) while with your other hand under its belly, support the fish's weight, making sure you don't squeeze, and at all times keeping its body in the water. Turning the fish upside down will usually stop it from struggling. And whatever you do, keep your fingers away from the gills. They are the most fragile part of the fish, and are easily damaged. Any bleeding from the gills caused by mishandling is extremely bad news for the trout.

If you really want to lift your catch-and-release game to another level, decline the offer of your guide or mate to photograph you with your catch. The trout will be grateful, though, like its fight, the gratitude will be of a silent kind. If you think about it, for trout's sake, do you really need a picture of every fish you catch?

Ultimately, the arguments for and against catch-and-release are unwinnable, and it is a measure of the polarity caused by this issue that, for example, in Germany, catch-and-release has been completely banned. Considering the urbanised fishing they have there, maybe it is just as well. Here, as voluntary custodians of some of the last great places to fish for wild trout, we need to keep a broader view of things, and proper catch-and-release needs to be a part of this perspective.

Whether to catch and release or catch and keep is a personal and moral decision, and once you arrive at it you don't need to defend it one way or another. If you are reading this, chances are you've already made certain moral choices, such as not using worms to reel the fish in by their intestines and rejecting treble hooks because of their innate cruelty. For his part, Michel is adamant that whatever our own preferences and decisions, within the 'brotherhood of the angle' we shouldn't dish out easy judgement on others but respect each other's choices, as long as they are informed and carried out with respect.

To this end he cites the antediluvian story of a failed catch-and-release, which changed the history of the nation.

'On a South Island river, I got talking to this Maori guy, clearly a Mainlander,' he recounted. 'He said to me: you know the legend of how Maui was fishing, sitting on the bow of the big waka that is the South Island, and how he hooked and pulled out a huge stingray that would later became the North Island?'

'I've heard about it,' Michel replied.

'You know what, bro? He should have put it back, eh!' the Maori angler exploded with jovial laughter.

'No, mate,' said Michel who had made the North Island his home. 'Good that he didn't. That stingray was definitely a keeper.'

I believe that choosing a pet — especially if it is to be a companion with which you intend to spend a lot of time — needs to be a two-way process. You choose, but you also get chosen.

On the way home from Taupo I detoured through Ashburton to pick up my new pup. I already had a name for her — Maya — but how to choose one from among the almost identical eleven? They were all impossibly cute, playful and totally at ease with people, to the point that each sought human contact above fraternising with its own kind. This, I realised, was due to the extraordinary amount of time and care the breeder, Cheryl Whall, and her apprentice Rachel had invested into these furry little devils at the most formative time of their lives.

I sat the whole day with the pups in Cheryl's garage, which she had converted into a kennel and a dog kindergarten. The pups played, rolling around on the concrete floor like head-to-tail fur balls. They ate their food and fell asleep on top of each other. They tugged at my shoelaces, nibbled at my fingers with tiny teeth as sharp as cats' claws, and still I could not decide.

But I realised that my being there, available, was part of the process. I believe that choosing a pet — especially if it is to be a companion with which you intend to spend most of your time — needs to be a two-way process. You choose, but you also get chosen. And so I waited, though I couldn't help remembering that with Mops, who was born on my birthday, we fell for each other as if there was no one else around. Nothing like that was happening here.

In the end, I almost went for the litter's runt, who, though visibly smaller than the rest, showed extraordinarily stalwart spirit and courage, picking fights with everyone, including her own parents. But Runty was a little too full on, too do-or-die, though later I learned that she had completely changed and settled, once away from the rivalry of her siblings. At one point that evening I looked down at one of the pups asleep on my lap. Earlier she had given Runty a hearty send-off, but now she was happy to chill. I patted her and she stretched without opening her eyes, trusting and relaxed.

'Hey you purebred mongrel, it looks like it's you and me,' I thought to myself as the pup stretched again, then going limp on my lap, started to snore. It seemed we had both made our choices.

Cheryl gave me a cat box to contain the pup during the long drive home, but the little hell-raiser would have none of that. For three hours I drove to the sound of unceasing cries and yelps, barks trailing off into yawls, howling ending in crescendo barks.

'She will tire,' I told myself. I could not give in to the tantrum. That would set a precedent that she could get her way by simply terrorising me with noise. In this battle of wills I had to be a clear winner. Now and for the rest of our days. Amen.

But she would not shut up. In Tekapo, two hours away from home, I stopped to get out of the camper and to rest my ears from this mournful cacophony. I let the pup out of the box and into a fishing crate, in which I usually carry my waders and wet boots. She'd have more room in that, and fewer reasons for protestation.

By the time I came back she had somehow managed to climb out of the crate and was exploring the camper's bench, which folds out into a bed. 'Fine, you can stay there if you want,' I said, feeling I was already losing ground and authority. As soon as I started driving, Maya crawled forward, squeezed herself between the front seats and clambered onto my lap. There she curled up and was soon snoring, and twitching, and running in her sleep, and the rest of the journey home passed in blissful silence.

We were getting to know each other.

August

IN EARLY AUGUST DAVID WAS BACK AGAIN
in New Zealand but this time his agenda was different.
It was the heart of winter and he was coming to ski,
bringing all three of his teenage kids, usually scattered around
far-off universities. This was a family affair. A comfortable lodge,
après-ski, gourmet dining, not our usual roughing-it kind of trip.
Still, he couldn't resist asking over the phone: 'Shall I bring my
rod, you know, in case the snow is not so good?' The snow was fine,
I told him, 'but definitely don't leave home without your stick.'

'But . . . is it worth it, the fishing at this time of year?' It could
be, I replied, trying to sound neutral. He didn't know, and I did
not want to spoil the surprise. If you think the skiing is going to be
good, I thought to myself, the fishing is going to blow your mind.

Usually, come the end of May, even the keenest of fly anglers put
their rods away until the spring. Unnecessarily so, because winter
fishing in the Lakes District — from Wanaka through Wakatipu to Te
Anau — can be as good as in Taupo. As I've said, I enjoy travelling

to the volcanic region for a fix of its trout and ambience, but it is four days' drive there and back, and always a hit-or-miss venture: when you hit the runs it is fabulous, when you miss them it is absolutely dead. One year, I decided to stay home and explore the local waters, and — surprise, surprise — I found plenty of fish and not a picket line in sight. Sure, the fish are a little smaller than the Taupo average, but they still reach a respectable 3 to 4 lbs, with a few sixes and sevens if you're lucky. In any case, landing a 4-lb rainbow in big water like the Clutha River is momentous enough to make your arms tremble for a while afterwards. Because the water is cold — often straight off the snow and the glaciers — the action can be electric. In fact, when you touch a fish which comes from a glacial river, your hands go numb within seconds. It's as if touching a trout could give you frostbite.

Winter in the Lakes District is mostly about skiing. The Austrian and the US national teams come here to train, and from around the June solstice to early October the morning rush hour consists of one-way traffic streaming up the mountains. Around Wanaka and Queenstown you see a lot of people sporting the bug-eyed suntan that comes from spending long days in the snow, and at night the lights of the snow-groomers make the ski fields look like distant Christmas trees.

Fishing is certainly one of the last things on people's minds, and yet, over the past fifteen years during which I've lived in Wanaka, I've come to consider skiing and fishing as complementary winter activities. After each fresh snowfall, when we chase the elusive powder snow, the rivers are usually in spate and unfishable. Then, after a few days of skiing, when the quads burn and the body aches, the powder is all tracked out but the rivers have cleared. A 'fresh' gets the fish moving, and just after it recedes is an ideal time to catch them.

I love this way of fishing. After the intensity of summer hunts, the long walks and even longer returns, here is a way to relax, fish side by side with mates, enjoy the scenery, ponder the meaning of things a little.

The first day with David and the kids we skied Treble Cone in Wanaka, and when in the early afternoon their legs refused to carry them any further, I suggested my long-prepared alternative. 'Let's go down and fish a bit,' I offered. 'No point burning your legs out on the first day. You've got a whole week of this.' They agreed.

We drove to the nearest river mouth, and David and I pulled on our neoprene waders and walked out to where the river and the lake met. The kids played on the beach, building a driftwood bonfire, and we began to fish. The lines were running vertically down over the drop-off from our rod tips when, twenty metres out, a solid rainbow jumped, flashing quicksilver. I stripped my line a little and it moved freely. 'It must be you, David,' I said. 'Tighten your line.' As he did, he came across resistance, then with a jolt that nearly pulled the rod out of his hands the fish jumped again. 'Holy shhhh . . . !' he exclaimed, fumbling with the reel. And then it was on — fish on, reel singing, rod held high. I felt a solid take, struck and missed. Doesn't matter, I consoled myself, there will be more. And there was. Later, in-between fish, I described to David the nuts and bolts of this fishing style which I had transplanted from Taupo.

In winter, because there is virtually no visible insect life, you have to fish deep, using streamers and egg patterns. Essentially, you are fishing for spawning rainbows, which linger around river mouths to gorge on ova and fingerlings washed downstream and into the lake. In the Southern Lakes district, brown trout begin their spawning as early as late March and continue well into winter. Once in spawning mood, they pair up, their bodies turning dark — almost black — and become completely unresponsive to an angler's offerings. Rainbows, on the other hand, continue to feed voraciously throughout their spawning.

Choosing where to fish in winter is simple: you need a river mouth with a well-defined drop-off that is within casting range of where you can safely wade. Stay at least a rod length back from the drop-off as, being made of sediment, it can suddenly slump and deposit you in the drink, which at this time of the year is only a few degrees short of iceberg temperature. Also, the fish often patrol the very lip, and you can spook them by coming too close.

Some of the larger rivers, like the Clutha, are also open to fishing, and there will be trout wherever there are good spawning beds. A recent Fish & Game helicopter survey along the Upper Clutha revealed the highest fish densities in recent history. However, the fish are not evenly distributed throughout the river, so a bit of local knowledge or the methodical sampling of different areas is essential.

The most vital part of winter-fishing equipment (apart from neoprene waders, because you won't last half an hour in your Gore-Texes) is a fast-sinking, or better still a shooting-head, line. The latter is unlike any other fly line. It is extremely heavy and only about ten metres long. The rest of it is braided backing, the stuff knotless loops are made from. To successfully cast a heavy line you also need a stripping basket, which prevents the coils of line from sinking before the cast. Powerful but slow-to-medium action rods are also preferable as a fast stick does not give the line enough time to straighten, throwing all sort of kinks and kicks into it.

The tricks to casting a shooting head line are having the backing nicely coiled in the basket, loading the rod to its full power and not having too much line in the air during false casting. If your line hand is near or on the line-to-backing connection, it's about right. After a couple of false casts, once the rod is fully loaded (ideally with a bit of double-hauling) you simply shoot the line forward, allowing the backing to follow out of the basket. I tend not to let the line go out of my line hand entirely but make an extra rod ring with my thumb and index finger. This guides the backing and helps to avoid tangles. Also, make sure you have not waded so deep as to have water at the bottom of your stripping basket, as this messes up the coils and turns the backing into a bird's nest on subsequent casts.

With all of the above going smoothly, you can cast thirty-plus metres without too much fuss. Mike Weddell, a former world casting champion, once told me that all of the long-distance records are achieved with shooting-head lines, with the top guys reaching the eighty-metre mark. For our purposes, such distances are unnecessary. If you can get your line out twenty metres you're already fishing. Most of the takes happen during the last third of the retrieve, anyway, when the fly is right on the drop-off.

After the cast, you need to wait until the line sinks all the way to the bottom, before beginning to strip it into the basket again. It is imperative to match your stripping action to the type of fly you're using: eggs, for example, do not swim but are entirely at the mercy of the current, while smelts and Woolly Buggers dart in short, fast zigzags. If your egg swims about vigorously it may elicit a few curious glances at the bottom of the lake, but not much else.

It has been my experience that fish fight differently, depending on what kind of fly you hook them on. The difference between a hook-up with an egg pattern and a smelt is enormous. In drop-off fishing, eggs and eyed ova flies, from glowbugs to Boobies, are the most deadly imitations because all the naturals from the entire river system wash up at the river mouth, which is where the trout waits for them. However, fish taking egg patterns often hook themselves in the soft parts of the mouth and not the cartilaginous lips. The resultant combat is usually short and uneventful, with the fish giving in easily. The same fish hooked on smelt is an entirely different kettle. I've had a 4-lb rainbow bouncing off

Woolly Bugger

the surface six times like a basketball, each jump getting a metre of hang time, before it dived for the bottom and sulked there for minutes, immovable like a brick. And that was not the end of it, either. Whatever the fly, keep in mind that in this style of fishing the trout usually hook themselves hard. With the inevitable big hooks, releasing the fish involves a fair amount of dental surgery. Unless you fish to eat, using barbless hooks in drop-off situations makes a lot of sense.

We certainly fished barbless, and the trout that occasionally got off the hook only added to the excitement. I can still see David on our last day together, braced against the current of the Clutha. We had skied hard earlier in the day, from mid-morning, when the snow had softened, to early afternoon, when it become too slushy, then left the kids up the mountain to catch the end-of-the-day shuttle. They were booked in for snowboarding lessons, so we knew they'd be 'stoked'.

We bee-lined for the river, and David was already casting before I could put on my heavy waders. From the plentiful driftwood I made a small fire and set out a pair of camping chairs around it. I lost count of the fish we caught, but it must have been well over a dozen, all magnificent rainbows in fast, frothing current. And, still, David kept hooking into them, one after the next, and I left him to it, knowing that I was witnessing his lifetime memory in the making. The sun dipped beyond the Pisa Range and the darkness came down rapidly. The temperature plummeted, I edged closer to the fire, and topped up my whisky glass.

'Just one more cast,' I heard David plead as he unhooked another fish. Sure, have a few more, I thought, watching the last of the sun gilding the snow on the highest peaks. Get them while you can. There was a forecast for heavy snow. Time to swap the rod for skis again, if only for a few days.

That August the fishing–skiing idyll came to an abrupt end. It seemed that the spectre of industrial development was spreading to overshadow trout waters everywhere. Even my home river, the Clutha, was not exempt from the corporate onslaught. Worse, it had once again become a primary target.

Every time you travel along the Clutha, there is an inescapable sense of two distinct histories, a kind of biblical déjà vu: the time before and after the flood. The deluge was brought about when governments in the mid-1900s decided to put the river to work churning out megawatts.

Ten concrete shackles were originally planned for the Clutha, though fortunately only three eventuated: dams at Roxburgh in 1956, the outlet of Lake Hawea in 1960 and Clyde in 1992. Two-billion-dollar Clyde, the grandest in the scheme, caused widespread protest but was still brutally forced down the country's throat. With scant regard for its environmental implications, it was promoted as a necessary evil for the common good: power for the people. (Later, former Deputy Prime Minister Michael Cullen admitted that the Clyde Dam was 'the single most monstrous environmental sin over the last thirty years'.) Were it not for HOWL (Hands Off Lake Wanaka), an outspoken community movement, there would have been another dam at the Clutha's very source, and neither I nor any other angler would have been able to call it a 'home river'.

Now, with the lessons of the past forgotten or conveniently ignored, more dams were planned for the Clutha, together with demands for greater water extraction. At one meeting debating the river's future some home-grown environmental luminary voiced an opinion that all that river water going out into the ocean was a wasted resource. It was a clear example that what for one person is a beautiful forest for another was an equally beautiful stack of timber. Against such myopic visions, along the Clutha another howl of protest was gaining strength. People were networking and gathering in numbers against more environmental monstrosities. At the centre of it all was another defender of wild, free-flowing water: Lewis Verduyn. Like me, Lewis considers the Clutha his home river. Its muscular current seems to be coursing in his own veins, a not impossible scenario considering that his beloved river once nearly claimed his life.

At Lake Wanaka, the source of the Clutha River, Lewis once had a dream, a longing for a time-travel experience. It was to be a quiet, home-grown adventure, without sponsors' flags flying from the masts and corporate logos patching his rafting shorts: an explorer's voyage, bold in spirit and Heyerdahlesque in scope.

The idea itself wasn't new. In the 1860s, a small group of daredevils with a penchant for mixing business and adventure had established a profitable, though dangerous, timber-carting route from the forests of today's Mt Aspiring National Park to the treeless and timber-hungry settlements of Central Otago. The link between the two was the Clutha River, the largest river in the country, which the men saw as a smooth and reliable high-speed conveyor belt, only sporadically buckled with rapids and hairpin bends.

The men would buy logs from the sawmills of the Matukituki and Makarora Rivers, lash them together into rafts, then pole their unwieldy crafts into Lake Wanaka. There, they would assemble the individual rafts into floating islands of timber, rig them up with square sails and, helped by the prevailing north-westerly winds, ferry them across the lake to the outlet of the Clutha.

It was here that the conveyor belt began, where the entire lake funnels into a river. The raftsmen would again split up the logs into smaller rafts, outfit them with rowlocks and eight-metre sweeps, and push off into the current and the crux of their journey. From its outset the Clutha flows clear and fast, and the men could make the eighty-river-kilometre voyage to near Cromwell in a day. They had to negotiate major rapids like the Devil's Nook — a notoriously destructive dog-leg corner — and the Boiling Pot, where the current warps upon entering Maori Gorge. The river could smash their heavy rafts like matchstick toys, so the men, accustomed to losing and salvaging their precious cargo, often preferred to walk the banks and ease the rafts on ropes down the most difficult stretches. The first time they attempted to run a log raft beyond Deadman's Point, in Cromwell, the craft turned a complete somersault in a rapid known as the Gap. After that, they thought it prudent to land at Lowburn.

There they would dismantle their rafts and sell the timber. They would stay the night at the local hotel, and at first light return on foot to Wanaka, some fifty kilometres away, carrying the coils of their hemp ropes. The same afternoon they'd construct another set of rafts from logs that awaited them at the lake's outlet, to be ready to push off the following dawn. Thus three Clutha trips a week could be done, and although several men lost their lives on the job, for the raftsmen the returns and the adventure outweighed the risks. 'It was strenuous work,' wrote one of those good keen men named George Hassing, 'but we were young . . . and delighted in it.'

Such was the inspiration that fired Lewis Verduyn's dream: to build a log raft, retrace the pioneers' journey and then extend it all the way to the sea. He wanted to taste their hardships and relive the peril. And in this the river would not disappoint him.

His first five-tonne Oregon-pine raft, called *Destiny*, which he constructed in Makarora, was swept away by an overnight flash flood only two days into the trip and was never seen again. Lewis, however, already an experienced rafting guide, would not be so easily deterred. He built a second raft — seven logs and four braces lashed together with 200 metres of natural-fibre rope — which he poled and sailed to Wanaka. There, after some dry-dock repairs, he navigated the raft out of the lake and into the Clutha.

During the different legs of the journey that followed, Lewis was joined by several able-bodied mates, and together they poled, pulled, pushed and steered the raft around innumerable obstacles, and sometimes simply held on for a bucking-bronco ride. The lumbering *Destiny II*, an eight-by-three metre, four-and-a-half-tonne plaything for the river, was repeatedly stranded on shoals and snagged against the low-hanging willows which in white-water parlance are called strainers. It capsized more than once and was righted again by skilful manoeuvring into the rocks and current and, on occasion, with the generous help of local farmers, their horses and a tractor. In the Cromwell Gap it turned into a submarine after hitting a giant stopper wave. The river closed over Lewis, spread-eagled on the deck, for what seemed like a breathless eternity.

Finally, 440 km and fifteen river days after leaving Makarora, Lewis nursed his battered raft into the ocean and a beach landing. He had fulfilled his dream, and in the process got to know the river so intimately that an unusual bond formed between the two. The voyage of *Destiny II* took place in the summer of 1981–82, and Lewis has lived to the rhythms of the river ever since.

No surprise, then, when I first met him in his riverside cottage — fittingly, the former residence of a ferryman — that we talked river for hours, two aficionados sharing their memories of an old friend. Like the pioneers he emulated, Lewis has combined both adventure and business into a river-based lifestyle, an eco-rafting venture focused not so much on white-water thrills but the broader riverine environment. He had just completed his twenty-fifth rafting season. This called for a celebration, one last trip of personal thanksgiving to the river for its season of plenty. He invited me to join him.

The Clutha's quiet but formidable power comes from its large,

> *Wherever there were patches of fine gravel I could see pods of spawning rainbows jostling, shuffling, holding resolutely in the current.*

high-rainfall catchment area. Figuratively speaking, the river is like the trunk of a giant tree with a broad, spreading root system. Three large lakes — Wanaka, Hawea and Wakatipu — anchor the roots into the foothills of the Southern Alps, but their extremities penetrate as far as Fiordland and Haast. The Greenstone, Caples, Rees, Dart, Routeburn, Wilkin, Young, Makarora, Matukituki and Hunter rivers all contribute to the Clutha, whose total catchment extends over some 20,582 square kilometres.

Even in the world of large rivers — the Amazons, Yukons and Yangtzes — the Clutha still places in the top twenty when the volume of water is considered. The 338-km Clutha is not especially long, as rivers go, but it flows at a dizzying speed. This haste was apparent as we put in Lewis's grey inflatable raft at Albert Town, near the first bridge spanning the river. The boat picked up speed instantly, moving at fifteen kilometres an hour without a single oar-stroke. The water was clear as air, and I could see the rocks on the riverbed three or four metres below rushing past like a landscape through the window of a train. Wherever there were patches of fine gravel I could see pods of spawning rainbows jostling, shuffling, holding resolutely in the current. They'd scatter at the sight of the overhead danger and just as quickly regroup after we passed.

Superb water clarity is one of the Clutha's outstanding features, Lewis told me, the result of the decanting effect of its sources. 'Lake Wanaka acts as a sediment pond for the glacial silt, and then the top layer of spring-pure water is drained off by the river,' he said. The Clutha is 'ninety-nine per cent pure, one per cent gold,' he likes to quip, referring to the river's gold-rush days. Even today, whenever you wash a handful of graphite-grey river sand in a prospector's pan, you'll find flecks of gold glittering in the troughs of the corrugated-bottom dish. They are as fine as overly ground coffee, and feel buttery when you rub them between your fingers.

On this winter day the river gleamed like a plait of greenstone set in grey. For now there were no thrills, no rapids or drop-offs in sight, but the satin-smooth surface belied the river's power.

The raft's paddles, I noted, were stowed away, and Lewis used only a pair of oars, which he controlled from a seat on an elevated centre frame. The frame had muffled oar rowlocks and was built from bull-bar-like tubing, streamlined not to catch on rocks or branches. Underneath the frame, the raft's catamaran-like hull was soft and flexible, able to pour like water over the surface of obstacles. Oar rafts are rare in New Zealand, Lewis said, but they are standard on big overseas rivers like the Zambezi and Colorado. 'You could never get away with a paddle raft on a river like this unless you had a coordinated and responsive crew, and you can't expect novices and tourists to become a team within minutes of putting in,' he said. 'I encourage people to paddle, so that they can feel the strength of the current, but I retain full control over the raft with the oars. I guide the raft, but the river guides me. That's the secret of safe rafting. On the Clutha, you cannot afford any mistakes.'

Most of his passengers assume that because there are no big rapids, there is no danger, Lewis went on. 'They don't realise that it is the flow of the river and not its white water that is the greatest threat. The water pressure is about a tonne per cubic metre. So they enjoy the cruise and the scenery unaware that if I were to misjudge a turn, we could all be swimming in two seconds, perhaps dead within minutes.'

I watched how he steered the raft. He walked the oars with measured crank-handle spins, pirouetting the raft casually, aligning it with the current, making the most of the river's intricate flow patterns. He craned his head to scout the route ahead, but his controls were relaxed and understated, an unspoken testimony to more than two decades on the river. Only when he allowed me a turn at the oars on the Pioneer Rapid — the biggest piece of white water on this part of the river — that I got a fuller appreciation of his skills.

We plunged into a set of standing waves that came at us like an express train, and I was fending them off, straining to keep the raft on course. The river yanked and wrung the oars, then jabbed them into my ribs, almost knocking me off the seat. For me this was like a scene from the movie *Deliverance*, but Lewis was sitting back, a relaxed passenger. He knew he was not taking any chances. The rapid may have looked boisterous and threatening, but it was also wide and free of obstacles. We would have got through it without any oar work at all.

Lewis took over just before the Devil's Nook, certainly not a place for a rookie oarsman. Here the river narrowed, sped up, then hit a cliff head-on, folding back on itself to create a fifty-metre whirlpool and a no-escape eddy. Picture the satellite image of a tornado and you'll get an idea of Devil's Nook: a twister of such centripetal force it makes the water look as thick as ready-to-pour concrete. But Lewis maintained his dance-with-the-river approach. He played the whirlpool so that the raft spiralled in its grip, now rushing at the menacing cliff, now being sucked back upstream. There were baby twisters regularly calving from this mother of all whirlpools, and Lewis craned his head, looking for an opportunity. Suddenly, he dug in the oars, locking into a breakaway vortex just as a surfer would catch a wave, and we were pulled out of the trap, spiralling into the mainstream.

Below, the Clutha flowed smooth again, fast but relatively benign, wild and free for many kilometres. Gliding down the muscular current, I could not even imagine it being stilled by dams, turned into a succession of long, placid reservoirs connected by spillways. I offered this thought to Lewis, who couldn't — wouldn't — see it either.

'The power companies are locked into this idea of endless consumption, an ever-increasing demand for more power and more dams,' he said, his hands effortlessly spinning the raft through a tongue of current. 'Of course they want more dams. They're in the business of selling electricity, and they want to sell as much as they can regardless of whether we need it or not.

'Dams are like dinosaurs. They wreck the landscape and they're headed for extinction. There are far better technologies to generate electricity now: marine, off-shore wind, solar, geothermal, even dam-less hydro. We have 17,000 megawatts of marine power in Cook Strait alone, and we only need 12,000 for the whole country. The future is in reducing power waste and using smarter technologies, not in building more dams. Besides, more dams will never solve our power problems. According to the industry's own figures, we'd need another Clyde dam every twenty-nine months. That's clearly unsustainable, because we are running out of rivers.'

We pulled out by the next bridge and loaded the raft on to a trailer which one of Lewis's associates had brought down. That night I paged through a book called *Who Killed the Clutha*, by Dunedin dentist Paul Powell, but I found both its title and the author's effort to dish out blame a misplaced effort. Ultimately, a river like the Clutha cannot be killed, nor could it ever be harnessed, confined or regulated because, like nature itself, the river is stronger than we may care to acknowledge, caught as we are in our technological self-aggrandisement. Consider the fact that the Clutha has changed its course many times during its history. In the distant past, as a retired Cromwell irrigation engineer once told me, it flowed into Lake Wakatipu and out of its southern end near Garston. During the largest recorded flood, in 1878, when its mouth shifted north and splayed into the present-day delta, the river left the entire town of Port Molyneux — planned as a facsimile of Dunedin, right down to having its own octagon — forlorn and dry. The river has worn out rocks, cut canyons and carved gorges. It was here before us, and it will outlast us, and a few lumps of reinforced concrete will not make a difference.

What is at stake, then, is not the existence of rivers like the Clutha but the quality of our own life with them. So far, the Clutha has been an unceasingly giving river. Its very flow is an act of giving. It has given gold, megawatts and irrigation, allowing fruit and wine and a good life in the desert of Central Otago. It has given trout and recreation, the thrills of boating and cooling swims, and those more ethereal qualities: beauty, serenity, inspiration and solitude. Perhaps it is time that, for our own sake, we give something back to the river, not from the fear of its loss or retaliation, but out of respect for what we have received.

Lewis Verduyn has learned first-hand both about the river's power and its benevolence. Once, out for a summer swim, he was caught in an eddy and almost drowned. The current sucked him under, and each time Lewis surfaced, he grabbed a lungful of air and swam for his life, and each time the eddy sucked him back down. Third time around, Lewis blacked out and lost consciousness. An eternity later, he felt his knees scraping against the gravel of the river edge and he regained his senses. The river had let him go. The same eddy which sucked him under had deposited him safely on the shore.

'I learned a big lesson that day,' Lewis told me. 'The moment before I blacked out, I turned back towards the middle of the river, and let myself go with the current. That saved my life. The lesson was: never fight the river — it will always be stronger. Over the years, I've grown to understand that the river has a life of its own. We can't tell it what to do. Actually, if we are wise, we listen to it. If you know and honour its ways, the river will repay you tenfold.

This payment, mind you, will not be in dollars or megawatts, and the electricity companies would do well to get this message sooner rather than later: water is renewable, rivers are not.

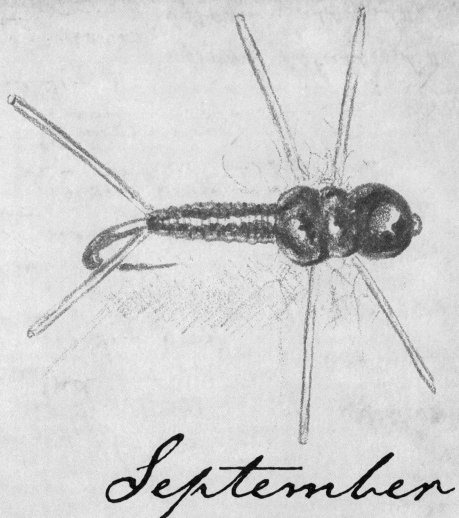

September

AT THE LAKES WHERE I LIVE, SEPTEMBER is the time of early-season still water, though I have to admit, for many years I was reluctant to fish it. Not that I was prejudiced against it, suffering from some obscure form of purism, favouring one type of water over another. In fact, I love the lakes. I live near two big ones, Wanaka and Hawea, and there are a host of others within an easy drive — Dunstan, Benmore, Wakatipu. So it wasn't access or the lack of proximity. It was just that, after the animated action on rivers, after seeing trout holding station against hard flow, darting across the current to take or inspect flies, I found still-water fishing — stalking the edges of lakes, not trolling lures or haunting river mouths — a little uneventful, and well, more than a little hard.

Sure enough, mile for mile I'd see a lot more fish along the lake edges than on any river. But getting them to take something, and succeeding, always seemed to me like a minor miracle. It probably did not help that my longtime friend and fly-fishing mentor, Wanaka guide Ian Cole, is a still-water specialist. Every time I'd go out with him, fish — nice fish, too — seemed to materialise out of the deep, black water that stretched beyond the drop-off, come into the shallows among the rocks, weedbeds and sandy patches where they were much easier to see, and they'd take our flies with amazing regularity. Every time I'd go back on my own, often to the very same spot (such as the famed but often hellishly hard Paddock Bay — Ian's favourite) I would soon become frustrated and disheartened by endless refusals and spooking.

But then something happened. A change of heart and fortune. One February day I was walking a dog along the edge of Lake Hawea when we noticed an unusual spectacle on the water. Seagulls were dive-bombing the surface with frenzied greed, and to say that trout were doing the same from underneath would not be much of an exaggeration. I ran back to my truck to fetch my tackle, and over the next thirty minutes caught six magnificent browns, any of which would make your day on a river. I never thought still water could be so good. Many times I've travelled long and far to seek quality dry-fly-fishing, and this, as good as anything I've ever found, was happening only minutes from home.

Needless to say, for the next two weeks I fished every day (you've gotta walk that dog, you know) until the cicada madness tapered off. The fly the fish took most readily was a Yellow Humpy, which is odd, considering it looks nothing like a swimming or drowning cicada. The trout cruised just under the surface, whisky-gold against the black-blue of the deep, and they moved with remarkable confidence, zigzagging from one bug to another. At times they moved so fast I had to run along the shore to keep up with them and cast. One fish refused my fly about a dozen times, yet each time I offered it (on the run to keep up, there was no time to change flies) the fish came to investigate. But, on the whole, refusals were rare. My first Yellow Humpy began to unravel after more than twenty fish.

The oddest thing was that after that unforgettable cicada summer I started to catch fish in still water consistently, no matter what season or style. I caught them on bully and damsel imitations in early spring, on generic Pheasant Tail and Hare and Copper-type nymphs later on, then on midges and manuka beetles, Black and Peacocks and water boatmen as the season warmed up. I even began venturing back into Paddock Bay, and if not quite 'slaying' the hordes of fussy browns that inhabit it then at least picking off the less careful ones with satisfying regularity.

So what was different? Maybe I raised my skill level just the right number of notches, or undid some still-water hex that had plagued me before. I'm not sure. But here are some distilled thoughts from a still-water convert. Like many good things, they are born from much frustration, questioning and time on the water spent with some of the best fishermen I've ever known.

First of all, you need to slow down to the pace of the water you fish, and with still water this means going *really* slow. In fact, you'll spot most of your fish because they are moving and you are not. Determine in which direction the fish is heading, then cast a long way ahead to intercept it. Do not cast at the fish or just in front of it as you would in a river. Three to four metres ahead is not too far.

Straighten the line and leader and let things settle. Then, when the fish is about a metre away, lift the rod a foot or so to animate the fly. After that, stop and let the fish take the fly. Unless the fly is a bully imitation, moving it more than once looks unnatural and often spooks the fish.

Go easy on the take. In still water, fish have plenty of time, so the action often happens in somewhat slow motion. Particularly with a dry fly, it is all too easy to strike before the fish properly takes it. Though purists like Ian Cole would disagree, for the rest of us mere mortals using small strike indicators may be helpful, especially in slightly corrugated water. Just make sure the indicator is not too close to the nymph. When you lift the rod to animate the fly, a simultaneous overhead movement of another object such as an indicator can spook the fish, or at least distract it.

If you haven't so far, try some still water next spring and summer. Beyond the initial frustrations and disappointments, there lie endless shorelines of opportunity to stalk some very nice fish. These shores remain fishable after even the most cataclysmic rains, and they are never crowded. I might see you there. I'm still dreaming of another cicada summer.

One evening in my cabin on the Clutha River David said, 'You won't believe what happened to me today!' He had just come back from fishing the edges of Lake Benmore with two old trout dogs, Ian Cole and Steve Carey. It was early spring, as brilliant and fresh as it was tempestuous. The rivers were blown out, but the still water around Wanaka and Hawea was phenomenal. Or so I thought until David came back from Benmore.

'I've never seen anything like this,' my usually composed and erudite fly-rod compadre went on. 'I was wading among these flooded willows and saw a solid brown trout no more than two rod lengths away. I unhooked the fly from the keeper and held it in my left hand, ready to cast, but the fish kept coming straight at me.' He stood as still as a willow himself, David explained, until the fish was a hand's reach away, near his left knee.

'I couldn't cast — I couldn't move, not even blink — so I just let the fly drop from my hand — a Black and Peacock Ian gave me earlier. It plopped through the surface, started to sink. The fish saw it, and you know what? He came and took it! It was unbelievable.'

His description of the fight that followed, and the near landing of the fish, while emphasising his own momentary incompetence, was a blur of expletives which drew heavily on slang descriptions of both male and female anatomy and the ways of joining the two together. Sifting through them, listening between the lines, I got the idea that there were obstacles in the water and low branches overhead, and that, *in flagrante* of the combat, the fish probably swam between his legs as well. The hook pulled out, the fish was gone but it did not matter in the least. There were others afterwards, many others, David said, all hooked within a few metres. It was clear that fishing Benmore still water was a close-range engagement. Intimate, man, *real* intimate!

I was intending to be on that trip, too, but had to cancel at the last moment after Maya ate a dead shag while we were fishing Lake Hawea, and was now having a violent bout of indigestion and regret, making the kind of noises a clogged-up drain makes when you begin to unblock it with a plumber's plunger. But I have heard much about Benmore ever since the Cole and Carey duo had their red-letter day out there, catching an untold number of sighted fish, most of them no more than a rod-length or two from their feet. Now, hearing David's tale I was truly intrigued. A few days later I managed to convince Cole and Carey to go back to Benmore. I reasoned that since the skies were now clear and the equinoctial wind had dropped — spotting fish in windy overcast is hard-to-impossible out there — we should see if another red-letter day was in the offing. It turned out they were both wondering the same thing.

Lake Benmore, dammed at its eastern end near Otematata, is the gathering of all the rivers of the Mackenzie Country: the Ahuriri and the Ohau, with its tributaries, the Twizel, the Pukaki and the Tekapo which drain the foothills of the entire Mt Cook range. What makes large parts of the Benmore shoreline so enticing to fish are extensive shallow flats — weeds, sand and stones — shaded by rows of old willows, some of which are flooded partway up their trunks, so that the shores are a maze of woods, inlets and bays which can be stealthily waded. Brown trout cruise these waters, cutting clear shadows over the sand, ghosting over the gravels, picking off snails and damsel nymphs, and, later in the season, patrolling the edges of reeds looking up for dries.

We drove up from Wanaka, Steve came in from Twizel, and together we motored across the lake in Ian's sixteen-foot Stabicraft, tied it to a tree and fanned out along the line of flooded willows. It is always interesting to fish with guides of Cole's and Carey's calibre, because no matter how hard you try, and how good you think you are, there is always a gap in skills and abilities which you're damned sure you'll never be able to bridge. David had noticed it, too. 'Every time you look at one of those guys they're either fighting a fish or releasing one,' he said. 'And talk about being intense! Cole fishes as if the world was going to end this afternoon, maybe earlier.'

'He's always like that,' I said. 'Casts with one hand, eats his lunch with the other. That is if he remembers to eat at all.'

I learned to fish from Ian Cole; I mean to really fish, beyond getting lucky while harbouring delusions about my own skills. This was back in the days when the world was young, we had few cares and we all felt invincible. Now, professional guiding swallows him up for the entire season, so I rarely get to see him between October and April. Fishing Benmore was like going back to those old days, but on new and unknown water. And there was still plenty to learn.

I kept close to Ian, always in earshot of his swishing Shark Skin line. I found that the best tactic was to wade out and work my way back towards the trees, which provided a good backdrop for spotting in an otherwise open and glary landscape. The pyramid of Mt Cook, white and glittering, was the only spike in the flat wrap-around northern horizon, though we rarely let our eyes travel that far. The fish were close, sometimes too close.

I found most of them around the bases of submerged trees; soft, slow-moving shapes against the golden bottom. At first, I spooked every single one with but a single cast, before I remembered you had to put the fly a good two or three metres ahead of them, on an interception course. Leader straight, rod tip down, it was then a matter of waiting for the line to settle and the fish to get closer. Then a slow lift of the rod tip to animate the fly. The fish would usually turn for it. It would not always take, but even a close inspection was exciting enough.

'You're fishing too long,' Ian admonished. 'Two or three rod lengths of line is more than plenty. Keep it nice and straight . . . oh, you bastard!'

That last comment was directed not at me but a fish which had just ignored his fly.

'There's one coming towards you,' he called. I had way too much line out and had to let the fish swim under it before I dared to pick it off the water and halve its length on the backcast. The B&P plopped, then bounced off the bottom as I lifted the rod tip. The fish went for it, then changed its mind. It continued on, took something else, suddenly and violently shook its head, then exploded out through the surface, the sun on the water bracketing it briefly with half arcs of rainbow.

What the fish took was Steve's fly, identical to mine, though apparently more appealing. The take was visceral in its intensity. You could see the reactions of the fish, read its body language: the slight tensing at the sight of its prey, the languid refusal, the tiny dust-devil of fine silt the B&P stirred as it hit the bottom. I turned to Ian to ask some silly theoretical question, but saw that he was already on the other side of another tree engaged with a fish of his own. There was nothing for it but try to keep up with the pros.

The mechanics of fishing still water are deceptively simple: sight the fish, cast well ahead of it, straighten the leader, give the fly a slight twitch as the fish approaches. The choice of flies is not complicated, either. The ubiquitous Black and Peacock, a small, thin damsel nymph, the odd Corixa (water boatman), even a tungsten Pheasant Tail works well. And though you may goof up a lot — and it is easy to do on such delicate water — you'll get a lot of opportunities to hook your fish. That is the beauty of still-water fishing in New Zealand: along a kilometre of good lake shore you'll see more fish than in a day's walk up most rivers.

It is a good challenge, too, refining your skills and precision, sharpening the reflexes and timing. After tackling good, honest still water like Benmore, you can take on any river or spring creek and hold your own. Then maybe, like some of us have started to do, you'll begin to favour still water over just about anything else.

As the day warmed up, we found fish were taking the first of the mating damselflies along the beds of reeds that jut out into the lake like small peninsulas. They porpoised out of the water to grab each mouthful, the sunlight catching their dazzling golden flanks. There was no doubt about the nature of this hatch. Coupled damsels skittered low above glassy water, red and blue, dainty and metallic.

'Every time I see this I come up with a new pattern, tie it and try it, and always go back to a blowfly, which works far more often,' Ian said as we wistfully watched the spectacle, the fish rising to a fast erratic beat. Ian had a beautiful 'mating damsels' pattern, tied with grizzle hackles and red Ultra Lace tube, and I had a deer-hair damsel dry, reddened with a felt pen.

In the name of research we bracketed the fish with two casts and two flies, the double damsel on one side, my deer-hair on the other. The fish took something and we both lifted the rods in unison. Mine was heavy with the weight of an angry trout. It was a small moment of glory, outdoing the old trout hound, and briefly I grew in stature, like a pufferfish about to burst at the seams.

'I can show you how to tie that deer-hair pattern,' I offered generously. 'Not that hard. I'm sure you'll be able to follow it.'

But it was a short-lived triumph, and as a scientific experiment it proved nothing. No other fish would take either of the damsels. We reverted to bluebottle blowflies, then, as a slight breeze extinguished the rise, to the fail-proof B&Ps.

By the time we nudged the Stabicraft back into the boat ramp, it was dusk and well past dinner time. On the way back to Wanaka I was sprawled out on the back seat, with Maya, totally spent, a warm, heavy weight against my legs. The day was done, and Ian was driving with one hand while he finally ate his lunch. It had been an epic outing, and though I was not quite sure what day of a week it was — red-letter or black — I still had that red felt pen to put things right in my own calendar of life.

A few days later Ian called me. 'Hey, I've done some research on damsels, scientific stuff, really in-depth,' he said. 'Now I know why the fish didn't take my mating-damsels pattern.'

'And why was that, Ian?'

'You see, I didn't think about it, but when you look up close the female damsels are actually olive green. Only the males are red. That's why the fish refused my pattern. It's tied only with the red Ultra Lace. Which suggests that both mates are males.'

It's not easy to outsmart a trout.

After much planning and a couple of false starts, it was finally happening. Craig Smith was making good on his autumn promise: we were going to fish in Haast during the prime time of the whitebaiting season. These last two words usually conjure up images of large sea-run trout entering coastal estuaries to gorge on the translucent little alevins, but from past experiences we knew better than to base our expectations on such an elusive quarry. They come and go like silver ghosts, and often the closest you can get to one of them is when you hear a whitebaiter say: 'There was a real big one here yesterday.'

Once, I even managed to cast to such a leviathan, running after it along the gravel bank of the Arawhata River, repeatedly offering my best-money-can-buy Silicon Smelt to the fish that sloshed and zigzagged just below the sheet-metal surface, leaving a trail of takes that looked like multiple rises. But it didn't take my fly and I didn't get another chance. No, this time around we would not be chasing phantoms (though, of course, we'd be ready if they materialised). On this trip we were happy to focus on the resident brown trout, big, resplendent and presenting their own set of challenges, though, thankfully, rarity was not one of them.

We arrived on the last day of September, the afternoon before the trout season's opening. The day was perfect, the forecast even better. The three of us had all fished here before, though never together, not in such a concerted effort, not with a large window of clear weather open over the Coast. Craig had so fallen in love with Haast that he had bought a house here, a classic West Coast crib, weather-beaten and rustic, with a shed full of nets, cray pots and ancient surf rods, all framed by a miniature Stonehenge of greenstone boulders, temporarily left behind by the previous owner.

The house, which was to be our base for the trip, was not quite the Ritz, but what a location! Walking distance to two major rivers and their combined estuary, surf thundering beyond the windswept bar shaped into a long sand dune, sunsets over the sea. That evening, David and I walked the bank of the estuary, rods in hand. The sea-runs were in there all right, vehemently chasing herrings which themselves were big enough to hunt whitebait. Neither of us had four or five-inch feathered lures, and the fish would not even look at anything small, so in the end we just watched and marvelled. The anticipation of what could be is often more titillating than achieving the object of desire itself.

The following day, as we fished the high banks of a local river, I was to learn one of the most important strategies I've ever come across in my experience as a fly-fisherman, but to see its value you first need to understand something about the nature of Haast.

It is one of the most interesting places I've ever fished. Some people here still muster their cattle on horseback — and riders have drowned in the process — and others lose their 4WDs in river crossings. Everything here is a couple of notches harder than it first appears. To wit, on one of our sighted fish I was faced with a long and 'draggy' cast and decided to wade in to better the odds. The river looked benign and only knee deep, so no worries there. Two steps in and the water was suddenly reaching the buckles of my chest waders. There was a 'false bottom' to the river, a mixed

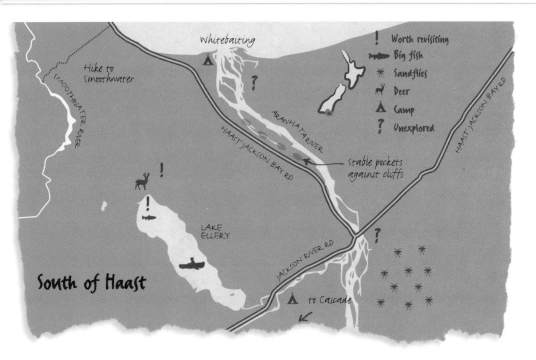

concrete-like layer of silt and quicksand on top of gravel. My foundering spooked the fish, and I didn't wade much after that.

The inhabitants of Haast still cling to the old nickname 'the Far Downers', as if to stress that in the search for their own promised land they went as far and as down as it was possible to go. I heard their story from Neroli Nolan, Craig's neighbour, who runs a lodge called Collyer House. One stormy evening during a previous visit, she stacked up the fire, poured out some good wine and took me on a journey back in time to the days when Haast was called the Wretched Coast, and its settlers, cheated and misled by a bureaucratic scandal, had to find their strength and forge their bush skills or die trying.

When the West Coast gold fields had been worked out in the late 1860s, thousands of people were without work, but the local government came up with an ingenious solution. It produced a prospectus about land in the far south. Any man over sixteen could take up a 10-acre section and a 50-acre block, and be granted ownership. The land was said to be fertile, covered with six feet of 'black chocolate soil that would produce almost anything', Neroli recounted, with gold nuggets littering the beaches and free passage to Haast offered on the steamer *Waipara* to all those who dared to become rich. Over 600 desperate people flocked to Haast, and none of them knew that the free tickets on *Waipara* were a one-way deal. On arrival, they found a land of sweat, tears and despair. There was no chocolate-rich soil as promised, but a swamp humming with sandflies and mosquitoes, lashed by biblical rains, bordered by the sea and cut by rivers of uncommon severity. Disillusioned people trickled out of the district by any means possible. Some bought their way out, others simply walked off the land. By 1927 the total permanent population of Haast amounted to nine families and four single men. 'The only people who stayed on,' Neroli said, 'were those who couldn't afford to leave.'

So you can see that Haast is a hard and harsh place and nothing here is easy, fly-fishing included. A peculiarity of the rivers here is that they are chockfull of logs. The apocalyptic floods, which rage down from the Alps and periodically turn the rivers into something akin to horizontal waterfalls, bring down enormous amounts of timber debris. Logs pile up like pick-up sticks over deep pools and outside bends. They make an ideal habitat for large trout . . . and a hell for the angler trying to catch them.

It was my turn to cast when we came across one particular fish, and, ever the optimist, I still had on a smelt imitation tied to a length of solid tippet. As I put the fly down, it bounced off the surface slightly and the fish burst out and took it in the air.

'Yay!' Craig applauded, 'I've never seen fish take a smelt for a dry.'

Hooking a fish, I knew, was the easy part. I looked around and saw trees everywhere and thought, 'Here we go again. It's like lassoing a wild horse in a forest.' This was when Craig yelled out his little piece of advice, though its significance was lost to me at first. 'Rodeo him!'

What?

'Rodeo him! Keep him splashing on the surface so his fins are in the air. That way he can't get any traction against the water. If he does . . . '

Oh, I knew all too well what happened when he did, when every square millimetre of his concertina-like fins found purchase against the water and its currents, when all his muscles, his entire being, were turbo-charged by the do-or-die boost of adrenalin.

One summer, in the course of a day on a nearby river so barricaded with fallen trees you'd think someone had introduced beavers here, and they nested and broke out into a plague, I hooked five fish all around the 8-lb mark. The cicada takes were electrifying. The fish would often ram the fly first, stunning the artificial insect, then back off to watch for a reaction. At this point, with my whole world coming to a standstill of anticipation, I'd give the fly a slight twitch, as if the bumbling insect was about to get away, and the fish would strike again, this time with its mouth open.

So far, so easy. The flies, brown deer-hair cicadas, were half the size of my thumb, and barbless, and the tippet, with nothing fancy required, was the 8-lb Maxima, as solid and dependable as trout tippets get. So what could possibly go wrong? Only one thing: the initial run seemed unstoppable, and at the end of the run each of those fish invariably found a tree to go under. The clever ones swam through entire root systems and weaved a couple of deft figure-of-eights around the tangle. The fly line would start to vibrate like a badly out-of-tune guitar string played by the current, and by this time, of course, the fish was long gone, having left me firmly fastened to a log jam. Only with one of those fish had I a glimmer of hope. As it took the fly I looked down and saw we had more than 300 metres of clear gravel, with not a snag in sight. 'You're mine,' I thought. Alas, no. Once the fish put its muscles to it, in no time we covered those 300 metres, below which there was the mother of all log jams.

Each fish was a variation of the same scenario, one replayed the following day and the day after. Hooking those large fish — and, by God, there were plenty of them! — was child's play, but in three days' fishing I did not land a single one.

Now Craig, who is a consummate backcountry adventurer, offered a practical solution to this quandary, not just theorising how it should be done but demonstrating it in action. You had to rodeo the fish, muscle it quickly, the way a cowboy brings down and ropes a cattle beast. Speed was of paramount importance if you were to take advantage of the trout's shock and confusion at being hooked.

In a nutshell, you could not give these fish even an inch of slack. From the moment of hook-up you had to keep the fish flapping on the surface no matter what, while your gillie mate jumped into the water and netted the brute. This was easier said than done, because the fish pulled so hard the rod tip was almost touching your reel hand. It was hard because it was counter-intuitive. By nature and from experience, you'd want to let the fish run, to tire it out, reel in just enough to keep a tight line and no more. But you could not cut these fish any slack.

The rodeo approach meant that the entire combat was over in a flash, which required coordinated teamwork and above all decisiveness and commitment on behalf of the netter. After a couple of bungled attempts we got the idea and the timing. It was obvious that no other strategy would work. Some of the fish we caught were living in pools framed on all sides by logs and sunken trees. Even a moment's hesitation, the tiniest bit of slack, was enough to let them find cover and snag the line.

The following days, benefiting from Craig's local knowledge, we explored a couple of little known spring creeks and found plenty of fish. Almost without exception they favoured their log homes, and without using the rodeo principle I doubt we would have landed any of them.

Walking back at the end of the day, I thought how the fish here were as hardy and resilient as any of the Coasters, and how anglers had to match and adapt to their ways. And I mused how, in an oblique sort of way, the West Coast government prospectus was right. The Haast region was indeed a promised land, but only if you loved the high challenge of fly-fishing for large and crafty trout.

On a riverbank in Haast, a man in green chest waders looked up from above his net, roused by my greeting.

'Any good?' I asked him, but he took his time to answer.

He looked me over from head to toe, and, finding no threat there, he turned his gaze toward my 4x4 camper. The sight reassured him. No telltale long poles, box frames or scoop nets.

'Tourist, are ya?'

I nodded. It was always easier that way.

'Naw, mate, nothing. She's quiet as,' he motioned to the river. 'We're all wasting our time here.'

I sympathised. Was it really so bad?

'Well, jokers up the coast been gettin' some, but here, naw. Rotten luck. Worst season in years.'

I suppressed a smile. I've been to the Coast too many times to take his woes seriously. The local credo was: ask no questions and you'll be told no lies. Still, I asked, and, dutifully, he lied. It was all part of the protocol. It was spring. The hundred-day war was on, the season of whitebaiting.

It comes every year, like Christmas, but it's even more anticipated, and far more serious. Already two weeks before the season's opening, whitebaiters arrive to set up camp, to claim the best possies, and to guard them against marauders, like me.

They are a tribe making its annual exodus to the coast to meet the migration of whitebait, and to go gaga over the translucent little fish that look like dabs of silicone window-sealer. They are all delightfully secretive, ready to lament the lack of luck, the misfortune of having the worst spot on the river, all the while using double-bottomed buckets to hide their catch.

Some come and go, others hunker down for the season,

Stu's 'rubber legs' nymph

erecting shanty towns of portable huts and garden sheds. Others live in caravans and campers with tarpaulin extensions. The sights and the ambience are nothing short of the gold-rush days.

A few years ago I found my own way into the tribe by fly-fishing for sea-run trout, which whitebaiters consider a pest. At first, the 'baiters were incredulous. Why would anyone run around with a fly rod when there was white gold to be sieved out and sold at $80 a kilo. But soon they granted me the status of a harmless eccentric. Then they began to volunteer information, and not just about trout.

The aristocrats among the whitebaiters own stands — gangplanks on stilts extending out into the river. In Haast, stands are the prime real estate. Each could fetch $10,000–$60,000, depending on location — if, that is, one ever came up for sale.

On the stand, the whitebait more or less catch themselves, though by law the owner cannot leave the structure unattended. This is a blessing in disguise for it offers the baiters a lot of leisure time. Each stand comes with a tiny shack attached to it, equipped with the bare essentials: a chair, a small table, a gas cooker, a chilly bin, and a small library of paperbacks: thrillers, westerns, and the ubiquitous Wilbur Smith.

'It's a good life, and you get to read a lot,' a man on the Okuru told me. 'Quality time of peace and quiet. All hundred days of it.'

I drove further south, down to my favourite spot on the Coast, the Arawhata gravel bar near Jackson Bay. At the mouths of rivers the ratio between reading time and hard labour changes rapidly. Here, the 'baiting is free for all, and the most active fishers prowl the river mouth right out to the surf zone, working it with their long-poled scoops.

I made a few friends at the Arawhata a couple of seasons ago, and I was thrilled to find them here again: Bill and Joy, Terry and Bev, and others, working the current with an unspoken clockwork etiquette. Though outwardly they appeared calm and relaxed, in their veins coursed the desire of compulsive players, not necessarily to win the jackpot, but to play and hope.

Presently, where the surf met the river, Josie, three days after her seventieth birthday, was straining against the incoming current, determined to make the most of her time at the coal face, the best spot in the line-up. You never knew if the next scoop might be the big one. After all, it was in the Arawhata that a fellow got 30 kg of whitebait in a single scoop.

Though the local lore is rife with stories of such sudden riches, it would be a folly to think of whitebaiting in purely monetary terms. Sure, they sell some of what they catch. But when you watch these people walking the banks, patient as herons, lost in the ritual of it all, it is clear their compulsion to fish is instinctual, almost genetic, as strong as that of their quarry. They may toil dawn to dusk, but at day's end they'll offer you a feed of whitebait, as Joy did on my first night in Arawhata.

I was reluctant to accept. They'd been working hard since 5 a.m., and the cupful of 'bait she offered was nearly half of their catch. But refusal, however polite, was not really an option. As night fell, I cooked the whitebait the purist way, folding it into stiffly whipped egg whites peppered with flour, to preserve the critters' delicate flavour.

A whitebait soufflé on a now empty beach, by a small driftwood fire, with bread and wine to mop up the pan. Starlight and silence broken only by the rasping of the sea against the gravel. Was it any wonder these people flocked here every spring? When I woke with the sun, the whitebaiters had already done two hours' work.

'I've caught the scouts,' said Bill, showing me the bottom of his white bucket, where several squiggly shapes snaked and milled about. Plenty of fish to start an aquarium, but nowhere near enough for an omelette. Still, the day was young, and so was the season. Last year they caught almost all of their whitebait during a two-day peak run. The pleasure was in not knowing which two days this would be.

I camped at the Arawhata bar for another two nights, whiling away the days in quiet contentment, hanging out with my favourite people — Crumpy's bunch in Crumpy's country. We read, and talked, and fished, and as the Okuru man said, it was quality time, every minute of it. Fly-fishing was the excuse that had brought me here, but for now I welcomed the fact that the fish were not interrupting us with their presence.

There was a spirit to my companions that I found earthy and refreshing. The little fish they were after, like my sea-runs, were important but not always essential. It struck me that in these days

of constant acceleration and information overload, when faster
is better, it was a good thing to slow down to the pace of a river, if
only for a few days. Or, in their case, a hundred days.

The whitebaiting tribe knows that, too, but, like most other
things, they keep it to themselves. No need to brag or elaborate.

On the way home I took a pee break for the dog and saw that our
usual pull-over spot was already occupied by another vehicle, which
had stopped for the very same reason. The dogs made fast friends
and I chatted with the man. His Terrano towed a trailer with a quad
bike, and the long handle of a whitebaiting net protruded from
under the ski rack. He was going where I had just been.

He enquired about the prospects, and I assured him they were
dismal, the worst in years. There was hardly any 'bait at all, and
sea-run trout were even scarcer.

The man nodded with empathy. Whitebaiting was certainly not
what it used to be. He wondered why he bothered himself.

Still, he called his Lab and they hopped into the cabin, waving
farewells, hand and tail. Undeterred, they headed for the Coast.

We both knew the truth. The season was as promising as ever. But
we had a tradition to keep. There was no need to state the obvious.

It is October again, and I thought I'd sneak a few early-season
days on my favourite River X in Southland. Excitement overruled
reason, however, and against the judgement of the cautious
weatherman in me, I drove straight into a southerly storm that
seemed like a reprise of winter itself. But the weather map suggests
that the front will pass quickly, and hasn't got much weight in it,
so on the riverbank I've nosed the camper into the storm and I'm
weathering it out. If the satellite maps are to be believed the skies
should be clear tomorrow, and for another two days after that —
almost more than you can hope for at this tempestuous time of year.

The waiting is not altogether unpleasant. I have a talking book
playing on the iPhone speakers, *Jennie* by Douglas Preston, and it is
read by multiple voices which create an impression of a theatrical
play. Maya is stretched out sleeping on the bench beside me, all four
feet in the air, and I have a half-full glass of smoky Clynelish single
malt on the table next to my fly-tying vice, with another finished
Audio Caddis in its jaws. The fly is as simple to tie as it is effective:
a black tungsten head on a #16 caddis hook, a few wraps of cassette
tape shiny side down, and two turns of grey ostrich herl behind
the head to complete the illusion. I like its spare, minimalist style

because it echoes my own new and distilled approach to fly-fishing.

After a year on rivers with some of the best fishermen I've known, and especially after a most enlightening trip with Marc Petitjean, I've pared down my trout gear, following the best I could their reductionist example. At its heart, fly-fishing is a journey towards simplicity, away from clutter and noise, towards places and states of mind that are pure and free. Reducing the fishing gear to the highest quality bare essentials is but a sign of a wider trend.

Thus I have dispensed with the vest hung with gadgets, its pockets filled with so many fly boxes some of them I'd even forgotten I had and carried. Now I have just one small chest-pack containing a big fly box with a hand-picked selection of *cul de canard* dries and nymphs, three rolls of different size tippets, nippers, CDC oil, knife. After all, a hunter does not need to carry bandoliers of ammunition. He or she is a sniper, not an artillerist.

I have packed all the rest of the gear into a carton box and labelled it 'Otamangakau' so that I remember to take it with me this summer when I go back to the lake and the whanau. I can already see Anaru's face when he opens this birthday present.

For me such spring cleaning has been good, too, like a de-cluttering of the space between me and the river, creating a more direct route to the trout.

The rivers have a way of drawing us in and holding us in their grip, both through their physical attraction and their mesmerising allure. If you've fished them long enough and with enough intensity you will know this to be true, without needing a genius like Schauberger to explain just how and why it is so. Rivers sharpen our perception, refreshing both body and spirit, washing away the grime of mundane existence. If they get deep enough into your blood, they begin to define your philosophy as well, shape your dreams, determine the kind of books you read and the issues on which you are prepared to make a stand and fight for.

In time, you may notice, as I have, that you are a different person from the one who stepped into a river long ago, clumsily waving a stick, hoping to catch a fish. But then, rivers can cut deep gorges and wear out entire mountains, dissolve and shape the rocks which are soluble, move those which are not. Why should they not be able to do the same with human minds and spirits, sculpting lives and characters, ideals and dreams?

Some people see their life as a series of sprints, zigzagging from one goal to another. For others it is more like a long-distance run, where the stamina and willpower to stay on course count for more than random flashes of brilliance. I like to think of life as a walk

> *I like to think of life as a walk up a river . . . Along the way there are riffles and pools, a scramble here, a crossing there, where perhaps you can offer a helping hand, or use one yourself . . .*

up a river, without undue hurry but with all senses alert. Along the way there are riffles and pools, a scramble here, a crossing there, where perhaps you can offer a helping hand, or use one yourself, all the while keeping your eyes on the flow and the mysteries that lie just below its surface.

Along this walk there are opportunities, like the sighted fish to which we can cast, and some of those are realised, and others bungled, and the overall tally does not matter so much as the fact that with each one we learn something new or understand better something we thought we already knew well. As such, we are here not to change the river but to be changed by it, and hopefully for the better. This would be my take on the meaning of evolution.

At the end of this river of life, in my mind's eye I see a large lake, still and tranquil, with plenty of shallows to stalk and trout that favour dries over anything else. I envisage a small cluster of fishing huts along one shore, simple log-chalet cabins, one for me and others for my river friends, those who have arrived before me, and others who will join us in due time. Mops will be there, too, and we will rejoin and rejoice as if no time had passed at all, and she will play with Maya as she would with a litter sibling, tearing up and down the sandy shoreline in that goofy Airedale fashion where the dogs' bodies take on the shape of question marks and their eyes are pure happiness.

In the evenings, if there are evenings there, we will all gather in one of the cabins and tell tales of the day's happenings, the how and the where, and which fly and which not. On this lake, there will never be any wind, only a gentle breeze to cool off the heat of the afternoon. The sun will shine from a cloudless sky, providing perfect visibility because the waters of the lake will never discolour.

In pairs and trios we will explore this lake, heavily peopled with trout, and maybe even salmon, until one day someone will find out that the lake is not, in fact, the source but that spring creeks and streams of crystal water feed into it from all directions, and that they, too, hold trout, and that they wind into the distant mountains, no one knows how far. And we will all hope that the creeks and streams go on forever, because we'll have an eternity to explore and get to know them.

This is the vision of paradise I pray to find at the end of the river of life. There will be other good things there too, of course: books and music and other such pursuits, though mercifully no television, and no bad radio and cheap advertising. Meanwhile, while the journey lasts and the river flows strong and clear, I do what I can to live this vision here and now. I cannot say I succeed at it all the time, or even most of the time, but, as with fly-fishing, successes and tallies have very little to do with what it is really about.

And so, paring down and de-cluttering my life the way I did with my fly boxes, I now live in a large caravan parked on the bank of my home river. It is the best real estate in town, with the Clutha not ten metres below, and framed by a belt of woods, above which there is an uninterrupted horizon of the Southern Alps, whitened with snow for much of the year. On sunny days, through my windows I can see brown trout cruising over the weedbeds of the big slow eddy below. The van has solar power with a backup generator, fast Internet and a miniature pot-belly stove called Little Cracker, which since its installation has become the heart and hearth of the place. This is my version of Thoreau's 'cabin in the woods', part of my attempt to live deliberately.

I fish most days now, even if only for an hour or so. When I walk Maya along the riverbank that stretches up from our cabin to the foot of the Dean's Bank and beyond, I often take a rod with me and try to outwit the few wary browns which hold in the eddies and feed lines peeling off the crumbling embankment. Sometimes there are rainbows among them, and these are often easy, new on the block and unaware of its dangers. When I don't take the rod I'm still looking for fish, and looking at them, and take great delight in figuring where they might be, and then finding and seeing them there. Those days I fish only with my eyes.

Reading this account of my fishing year, you might conclude that it was one long lucky streak of grand adventure, with no down times in-between. It was not so. There were times — many times — when absolutely nothing happened, times when we did not find a single fish, when a much anticipated rise never eventuated, or when, after a long drive, I arrived at the river to find it totally unfishable, twice its normal size and brown as mud. All this is part of fishing, probably a bigger part, but we've become such a highlights-oriented culture that even fly-fishing stories now have to have the sledgehammer pace of a thriller.

Real-life fishing stories rarely conform to the expected three-act structure of a hero facing insurmountable odds and challenges only to overcome them and succeed in the end. They are more about gathering disparate, often inconsequential morsels of information and wisdom, pieces that never quite add up to make a whole picture, because the picture is continually changing. As such, these stories often tend to be intensely personal and ultimately incommunicable to others, and would probably make for a boring read. Which is why, selective like an old trout, I've picked out of my diaries only what I hope to be of wider interest, paring down most of the mental ruminations fly-fishing so easily inspires.

At the beginning of this fly-fisherman's year I set out to find, explore and fish the best of New Zealand's trout waters, and this I've accomplished, though only to realise that for every location I've ticked off the lifetime list there are another three or four more, much less known and thus even more worth exploring. This has left me with a list longer than the one I started off with, a list full of places with alluring names like Manganuiateao and Kuripapango and others which I dare not even mention. They are all new to me, and coming to unknown rivers like these, if they are sufficiently different from those already known, is like arriving in a new country without knowing its language, customs, geography and currency. An exercise in exploration and learning certainly worth recording, and so I've already decided I shall continue this diary, in the spirit in which it was conceived.

With the stirring of the new season, my river friends are starting to return, their compulsive need to migrate back to their favourite rivers as strong as the upstream drive of a salmon. Smiley is back already, Grandpa Trout is coming for the summer, and I've just heard that, after his ordeal with necrotising fasciitis, Ross Millichamp is learning to use his prosthetic legs with such determination that he can walk a rocky riverbank already. Michel Dedual is planning a rafting trip down the Rangitikei, and the whanau are sending me text-message updates about the state of Lake Otamangakau. The year ahead is filling up fast.

The other day a ghost showed up at my cabin, and its appearance froze me in my tracks. For a ghost, he was looking remarkably well. Henry Spencer was thin, weak and slightly shaky, but his sickly pallor was gone and he said he felt so good now he has burned those letters he'd been carrying with him all season past.

'For months I've been living on borrowed time,' he said, 'and even that's eventually run out. And I thought to myself: hey, I'm still here, and actually feeling all right, better than I felt at the time of the diagnosis.'

He had made some radical changes to his lifestyle, he said: gone through a lengthy detox, flushed his body with pure water and liquefied green superfoods. As a man about to meet his Maker, he had also turned to matters spiritual, in the form of Taoism, which, curiously enough, has reverence for flowing water as one of its fundamental tenets. He had never believed in such remedies before, he told me, but what did he have to lose? Apparently, all was lost already. And yet this was the easy part, almost mechanical. Living as if each day was the last one was much harder. What kept him going mentally were the rivers and the prospect of spending even more time with them, he said. Rivers were both his therapy and the reward for pulling through.

His ordeal was not yet over, but the crisis seemed to have passed. One day, Henry said, he would get himself medically checked out, but not just yet. Whatever he was doing was obviously working; still being here was proof of that. All he would do for now was more of the same. Riverside therapy. Fresh air, pure water, long walks, and the happiness that looking for trout had brought him. And so we went to the river together again, on the pretext of hunting for trout.

Wild trout are many things to many people — food and quarry, embodiments of beauty and objects of desire, unknowable enigmas and an excuse to be near rivers. They can bring out the bad and the best in us, stirring up base instincts and flashes of spirituality. They bring about broken marriages and new unions, deepest friendships and heart-sworn enmities, and reams of literature in which *Homo sapiens*, stricken with trout fever, tries to find both existential meaning and an explanation of how it is possible that a cold-blooded creature can become such a dominating part of a person's life. Sometimes trout can give a person a reason to live when all other reasons fail.

If there is a common denominator in all this, it is that wild trout provide us with random moments of happiness, and we hunt those moments and collect them precisely because they are unpredictable. And as long as they continue to be so, we shall pick up our rods and head for the river, hoping to solve the mysteries of trout, knowing all too well that we cannot.